# *Where Have All Our People Gone?*

# *Where Have All Our People Gone?*

## New Choices for Old Churches

Carl S. Dudley

THE PILGRIM PRESS
New York

The figures on pages 5, 27, 31, 36, 38, and 87 have been reproduced from *Understanding Church Growth and Decline: 1950-1978,* ed. Dean R. Hoge and David A. Roozen. Copyright © 1979 The Pilgrim Press. The reader is invited to explore the fuller use of the figures as found in the original text; see pages 25, 257, 194, 107, 139, and 254 in UCGD.

Library of Congress Cataloging in Publication Data

Dudley, Carl S    1932-
    Where have all our people gone?

    Includes bibliographies.
    1.  Church membership.   2.   Church work.
3.   Christianity—20th century.   I.   Title.
BV820.D82        254'.5        79–525
ISBN 0–8298–0359–9

The Pilgrim Press, 132 West 31 Street, New York, New York 10001

*In appreciation*
*for two honestly different people:*
*Shirley*
*for whom believing and belonging*
*are as inseparable as faith and life*
*"j" (Joan)*
*who believes too much to belong*

# *Contents*

# *Introduction*

Membership decline for most mainline denominations, in the past decade, has been unexpected, unprecedented, and most upsetting. These mainline churches—Congregational, Episcopal, Methodist, Lutheran, Presbyterian, and Reformed—stand in the heritage of the great Reformation tradition. For the most part they represent the established churches that have dominated religious life in America for the past three centuries. This sharp downturn represents the first major reversal of membership trends since these churches began to keep records.

At the same time, some evangelical denominations continue to show membership increases. Today there are two million more Southern Baptists than there were a decade ago. Seventh-Day Adventists have increased by 35 percent; the Church of the Nazarene by 40 percent. In the same decade, the population increased by twenty million.

A wide array of denominational and secular research teams have probed these dramatic shifts in church membership, giving special attention to changes in church commitment since the end of World War II. This book evolved as one dimension of a larger research project, the findings of which are presented in a book entitled *Understanding Church Growth and Decline: 1950-1978.* This book reflects our concern that research should be reported in a way that is appropriate to the work of the local congregation.

I have not reiterated the work of the research panel, nor have I even tried to summarize their conclusions. Rather, I have presented significant findings in a format that should be useful to a pastor preparing a series of sermons, or a committee concerned about community outreach, or a denominational task force seeking to develop mission strategy.

This book was difficult for me to write, and at the same time it was very satisfying. The difficulties came in my efforts to be honest with the research information that others had gathered and organized. I brought a number of pet theories to the research findings in search of confirmation. I found a vast collection of information wider than my own experience and viewpoints that were quite different from what I had anticipated. Many cherished ideas were painfully abandoned.

The satisfactions came in finding names for experiences that had haunted me as a pastor, in finding reasons for awkward relationships that I did not understand. Working through this data has given me a new understanding of young adults in the church. I also found a new appreciation for church neighbors who willingly share in the life of the church but never join.

This material has forced me to confess my own biases: After fifteen years as a Presbyterian pastor, and now as a teacher and a participant with many different congregations, I know that the parish ministry is the front line of the Christian encounter. The effectiveness of any research, from statistical analysis to theological reflection, must be measured by its usefulness to Christian believers in our churches and in our communities.

At the same time, we do not start over with each new fragment of research or theological insight and try to rebuild the Christian faith ex nihilo. In the tradition of the Reformation churches, our studies included historical perspectives during the work of the panel and in the final collection of materials. As in my own faith and ministry, in this study I have sought to utilize the unique strengths that are native to the Reformation traditions in which we stand.

Membership statistics are not the only challenges facing the churches at this time; spiritual growth is at least as important. An impoverished world in need of bread and the Word claims the attention of the church. Studies in membership gains and losses are only one way to ask the larger questions of meaning, of the bonds between our beliefs and commitments, of the churches in which we serve, and of ourselves, personally before God.

This book is divided into two sections: first, a statement of concerns; then, a discussion of responses.

The first three chapters deal with the primary causes for dramatic losses in membership in mainline denominations: (1) the growing phenomenon of adult believers who have no use for organized religion, (2) the effects of increased mobility upon church membership commitments, and (3) the values of a generation of young adults who directly challenge the most sensitive tenets of the church as we have known it. I have concentrated on areas where strong statistical support is evident and have given little space to refuting popular but unsupportable theories.

Discussions of possible program responses are divided into four chapters, each progressively more specific. Strategies for evangelism are examined in chapter 4, and guidelines that seem particularly appropriate for mainline churches are offered. Chapter 5 explores the implications of this research for developing stronger worship experiences and programs in the congregation. In chapter 6 specific implications for congregational effectiveness in particular kinds of communities are suggested. The pastor's leadership is the subject of chapter 7. Finally, a chapter of summary, review, and suggestions for using this material is offered. An effort has been made to provide program implications with examples, rather than to develop an exhaustive list of program possibilities. Evangelism, church program, community influences, and leadership are the themes of these four chapters.

A mood of quiet excitement pervades several of the studies in *Understanding Church Growth and Decline.* Just beneath the surface of cautious, analytical, scientific inquiry lies a solid affirmation that these studies have, in fact, located the lost members of mainline denominations. They have not joined other flocks; nor have they rallied to the call of other shepherds. For the most part these potential church members are still in the community, but not in the churches. This book attempts to identify where they may be found and how they might be reached.

I wish to express special thanks to John E. Dyble, who shared this project with me from the earliest outline to the final copy. John checked and challenged the concepts, the application of research, the accuracy of tables, and the thrust of material as it evolved. Readers who are familiar with this book and *Understanding Church Growth and Decline* will appreciate the contribution he has made. In addition, I wish to thank those who have been members of other working teams over the past two years. Several have made a great many substantial comments, too detailed to enumerate, on the use of their research. A note of special appreciation goes to William J. McKinney Jr., of the United Church Board for Homeland Ministries; and the coeditors of *Understanding Church Growth and Decline*, Dean R. Hoge, of Catholic University in Washington, D.C., and David A. Roozen, of The Hartford Seminary Foundation in Hartford, Connecticut. Although I am grateful for their insights and suggestions, I accept responsibility for the form of the final text.

At least fifty pastors from Baptist, Christian (Disciples), Episcopal, Evangelical Covenant, Lutheran, Presbyterian, Reformed, Roman Catholic, and United Church of Christ churches, who participated in the Doctor of Ministry programs of McCormick Theological Seminary and of Lutheran School of Theology in Chicago, have made important contributions through their efforts to apply the research data to their congregations and communities. I value their open approach to learning as a time for seeking together, rather than for demanding previously packaged answers. In addition, I wish to thank my family, who revised our summer and our time together to make room for this project, and especially my wife, who makes it fun to live in a family of seven. Finally, I want to thank my New Believer friends, classmates, and neighbors for providing such lively models for this book.

# *Part One*

# CHAPTER 1

# *Believing Without Belonging*

"A quiet talk with a thousand Christians—that's what I wish I could have. I want to hear how they see the problem, one at a time." These were the sentiments of an exhausted church leader when he departed from a denominational task force to "deal with the membership problem." For this meeting, like so many in the past decade or more, the national staff had invited several celebrated pastors to help develop a churchwide program of evangelism. The pastors brought with them stories of membership growth in their congregations and their program recommendations for the larger church.

The stories were upbeat, and the recommendations added new frills to familiar patterns. But the meeting fell apart when the task force tried to write the first section of its report: the reasons for declining church membership. They had already agreed on a laundry list of program suggestions that might be tried in local churches, but they could not agree on why. Each person knew what worked where he or she was located, but collectively, their situations were different and their recommendations conflicted. Many in the group secretly doubted that the suggestions of others would work in their specific settings. They disagreed on the causes of declining church membership. But they skimmed over their differences, printed their

3

recommendations, and hoped that it would do some good, somewhere.

The discouraged leader lamented that there had been so much heat with so little insight. He wished he knew "what really happened to all those people who once were members of our churches." We have tried to provide an answer for his lingering question.

### *Church Membership Trends*

Churches were spiritually, emotionally, and physically unprepared for the roller coaster curves of church membership that have occurred since the end of World War II. Membership growth in the 1950s caught churches by surprise. Sanctuaries seemed too small; Christian education buildings seemed inadequate. Construction could not keep up with membership increases in existing congregations and in recently established churches scattered throughout new suburban areas. Straight-line growth projections were up. Churches overinvested in congregations, seminaries, camps, and other facilities to make room for the next generation.

Having overextended their credit to house expanding memberships, mainline churches were equally unprepared for the shaky statistics of the early 1960s and for the stunning decline in membership, which gathered momentum as the decade ended. Something happened to mainline church membership appeal and commitment. United Methodist church membership declined by more than one million in the past decade. Both United Presbyterian and Episcopal churches show losses of more than half a million members each. Membership in the Lutheran Church in America is off by a quarter million. For all these denominations the membership curves went up gradually, lingered briefly, and declined suddenly.

Although most mainline churches decreased during this

4

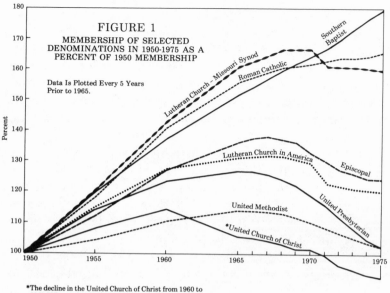

FIGURE 1

MEMBERSHIP OF SELECTED
DENOMINATIONS IN 1950-1975 AS A
PERCENT OF 1950 MEMBERSHIP

Data Is Plotted Every 5 Years
Prior to 1965.

*The decline in the United Church of Christ from 1960 to
1965 is due to withdrawal of congregations after the merger.

decade, other denominations that had stood at the edges of the
religious establishment continued to show membership increases and then dramatic membership growth. While most
mainline churches were going down, evangelical denominations kept pace with the growing population. Some were even
growing faster than the population. For mainline church
leadership the picture is familiar and upsetting.

Mainline denominations and academic institutions have
responded to this challenging new situation with all the resources of their arts and sciences. Statisticians collected data,
pollsters asked questions, denominational leaders developed
programs, theologians reflected, biblical scholars pondered,
pastors agonized—sociologists, anthropologists, historians,
missiologists, all took a look and commented. But church
membership continued to drop in the 1970s, then seemed to be
stabilizing, and now . . . the story is unfinished.

In the past few years mainline churches have declined while other denominations have increased in membership. Throughout these changes the affirmations of basic religious beliefs have remained almost unaltered in the American population. Recent Gallup polls suggest that Americans remain quite traditional in what they say they believe. Over 90 percent of the American population affirm that they believe in God. Nine in ten say that they pray to God. About eight in ten Americans believe that Jesus Christ was God or the son of God. Seven in ten say that they believe in life after death. Gallup poll data on these items has changed very little in the past twenty-five years. At the same time, mainline church participation has also fallen off. Regular church attendance is down significantly for the whole population in the past decade. Confidence in religious institutions continues to wane.

Americans are affirming religion, even traditional Christian statements of faith, but they are less apt to join mainline churches. Why Americans are saying Yes to questions on religious faith but No to invitations to mainline church membership is the subject of this book. In the words of one frustrated pastor, "Why are all our neighbors so friendly toward the congregation, and yet so few will actually join the church?"

### The Working Groups

In 1976 The Hartford Seminary Foundation, with the support of the Lilly Endowment, Incorporated, gathered a wide spectrum of denominational and academic researchers together to provide an arena for sharing their perspectives on the problem of church membership growth and decline. Participants brought different theological viewpoints and a rich assortment of professional expertise: pastors, teachers, executives, theologians, statisticians, sociologists, and historians. The resulting discussions were usually lively but rarely decisive. Although the approaches were varied and the conclusions different, the working group discovered a remarkably common base of research data. A portion of this information was shared with a much larger gathering of church leaders in a Hartford Seminary Foundation Symposium entitled "Church Growth and Decline: Implications for Evangelism," held in Hartford, Connecticut, February 1-3, 1978. Reaction to that presentation was so affirmative that Dean R. Hoge and David A. Roozen collected and edited the papers of symposium participants. These have been published by The Pilgrim Press under the title *Understanding Church Growth and Decline: 1950-1978* (hereafter noted as UCGD). Without their collection of current research, this book would not have been possible.

Hoge and Roozen have provided the most comprehensive resource of church membership information assembled in the past half century. UCGD includes a broad range of sources but has a relatively narrow focus: the studies are all concerned with membership growth and decline since World War II, in white mainline Protestant denominations. The questions asked and the responses offered clearly indicate that the studies, the commentary, and the insights are Wasp. They want to know what we know for sure, what we think is happening, what seem to be the causes, and where does it lead from here.

This book has a different focus: What does it all mean for the local church, the struggling pastor, and the concerned Christian? What appear to be the most compelling thoughts—positive and negative—have been gleaned from the larger body of research and are contained in this book. The statements find their support in the extensive studies of UCGD unless another source is specifically cited. In the text I have occasionally made reference to the work of one of the UCGD authors, noting the chapter where the expanded discussion may be found, for example: (UCGD, chap. 4). Under "Work Sheets for Church Groups" at the back of this book, there is for each chapter a section for discussion and response, made up of three elements: an appropriate Bible text for prayer and study, a variety of questions and suggestions for continuing discussion, and notations on the sections in UCGD where that particular theme is discussed in greater detail. UCGD also includes an extensive bibliography, which I have not attempted to duplicate. However, a few additional suggestions for further reading have been provided where they seemed especially appropriate.

The design of this book follows the title: Where have the once-loyal members gone? What choices must be made to bring new life into old, Establishment churches?

## *Unusable Answers*

From the beginning, let me dispel any notions that there are easy or obvious pathways that people have used to leave the churches. There are no mass movements in population statistics that explain the declining membership of mainline denominations. This is not a mass exodus from the old Egypt to the new Promised Land. There is no clear flow from one denomination into membership in another. There are no schisms that can account for lost members. No clear aversion to mainline churches has been announced, no anticlericalism to point out the problems. Although mainline churches are declining and some other denominations are growing in membership, there is no simple exchange of personnel. Even though these trends may be related, the individuals involved are not necessarily the same.

Some of the most cherished explanations do not hold up under close examination. Causal factors must be shown to influence church membership at the time and in the place when membership declined. Sometime around 1960 something happened in American culture. The result was a change in the habits of Americans but apparently not in their religious beliefs. What happened is the subject of widespread debate and disagreement.

*Wealth.* Some have suggested that Americans were too rich to be bothered with church attendance; weekends were occupied with alternative recreational opportunities. Wealth and leisure are often coupled as the twin monsters that have bedeviled church membership. Alluring as these options might appear (especially on a beautiful Sunday in midsummer), studies of church membership cannot support the thesis of worldly competition. Leisure opportunities long preceded the decline in church attendance and in no way parallel its configuration. If wealth and affluence make any difference in church membership, it is in the direction of increased church attendance and participation.

*Overwork.* Some have advanced the opposite argument, that people in the 1960s were too busy making money to have time left over for church activities. The increased employment included many more working wives, mothers, and church volunteers. Clearly, this cultural shift has had a direct effect on the programming for women's activities, in particular, and for voluntary activities, in general. However, an examination of church membership shows that the percentage of working-women (and multiple employment families) represented in churches is roughly the same as in the population as a whole. Something deeper and more pervasive was affecting the once-faithful members.

*Public events.* The dramatic and disturbing public events of the 1960s have been blamed for the decline of church membership. In an earlier decade the identification of a common enemy seemed to give solidarity to church membership: fascism in the 1940s and the Communist threat (in Korea, for example) in the 1950s. In the 1960s the divided public response to the Vietnam War may have triggered the opposite reaction to church membership. Among older Americans, fear of communism remains a factor of significant correlation to mainline church membership.

Further, the civil rights struggle involved the nation and

divided public opinion. Through the television tube, the drama of the civil rights movement of the 1960s entered every home, in the faces of frightened black children and the marching of their older brothers and sisters, in the shadows of locked university doors and shouts of Americans willing to do combat in the streets of their homeland. The disruption had significant social impact, but no single public event has been tied to membership decline.

*Social action.* In the midst of these disturbances, churches often appeared discouraged, divided in faith, and hypocritical in action. The effects of church participation—in particular, social action programs—are considered at length in Part Two. Although such activities have been a favorite target for people who seek a single cause for declining membership, there is no clear statistical basis to support that claim; there is no exodus of members, no clear coincidence of social encounter and church membership decline.

Voluntary institutions of all kinds experienced a decline in the 1960s; the scouting movement, social lodges, farm cooperatives, and parent-teacher organizations experienced similar drop-offs in membership. Certainly they were not all suffering from overinvolvement in social action. Beginning in the 1960s and continuing through Watergate, great masses of Americans doubted the authority of their institutions—political, community, familial, and religious. Something was happening not just in public events, but in the consciousness of the nation.

Whatever the precipitating events, perhaps all these and many more, the result was a shift of cultural values. Americans retained their basic religious beliefs but separated faith from institutional religion. Even though they continued to have an intrinsic appreciation of God, for many the extrinsic expression of their faith had changed. Both church membership and participation were seen as less important.

In the decade of the 1960s something happened in the private lives of many Americans that challenged and changed their values and their habits. For some it was an encounter with authority—draft resistance reached a peak in the history of the nation. For others it was an easy access to mind-changing drugs, a casual acceptance of sexual relationships outside of marriage, or an uncomplicated divorce. Attitudes and actions shifted radically during the sixties.

In that changing time, church participation no longer seemed as important as it once did. Individualism became a cornerstone of faith. Morality became a private choice. Religion became a way of personally integrating and interpreting life's experiences. Like marriage relationships of a former era, believing was divorced from belonging.

## The New Believers

For many people the church is the organized form of religion, and religion is the personalized expression of faith that is carried by churches. Religion and church are independent but inseparable. For many mainline church members, faith outside the church would be a rather shoddy second best. For conservative congregations, faith outside their own communion would be dubious, and even members of their own congregations are occasionally suspect. Those who remain outside the church are clearly "beyond the ordinary means of salvation." Believing without belonging is an awkward idea for mainline church members and a scandal to more conservative Christians.

As awkward and scandalous as it may seem to some, collected studies show that a great number of people find their religious faith apart from the organized church. Some who believe will join churches; others who believe will not. The opposite can also be said: Usually, nonbelievers have not joined churches, and yet, apparently, some have. The simple fact is, religious belief is not synonymous with church membership. Technically, this may have been true for a long time, but it is truer now than it has been for a generation, and the trend toward believing without belonging shows no significant signs of changing.

In spite of the religious boom of the 1950s, churches and synagogues have lost their franchise on religion. An increasing number of people appear to have meaningful and continuing relationships with God, much like contemporary "marriages," without benefit of clergy. From the perspective of mainline churches, bootleg religion is booming, and no repressive countermeasures seem to be able to stop the flow. It may not be Christian orthodoxy, but then "orthodoxy" depends upon the acceptance of institutional authority. Several studies show that many of the faith expressions of nonmembers were more articulate and often more steeped in Christian motifs than comparable statements from church members, many of whom seemed to assume that faith belonged to the church like a possession, while these New Believers claimed a faith for themselves.

Common grounds of faith can be found between believers, who belong to churches, and New Believers, who do not. These points of contact provide for simple appreciation of each other and for dialogue about their differences. One word of caution: Any identification of common ground is a risky, personal adventure. Mainline denominations cannot agree on content or priorities of their faith statements, even after three or four hundred years of dialogue. At the other extreme, the individual nonbelonging believer has announced his or her unwillingness to be lumped with others by the definitive nonaction of nonbelonging. After talking, reading, and listening to many people, this list is my impression of four common grounds across which both groups might engage in interesting, if not fruitful, dialogue:

1. *Personal religious experience.* Personal experience is paramount. In the point of contact, New Believers have joined the

great cloud of witnesses who have felt the power of God touch their lives. Experience is the entry into faith.

Personal experience is seen to precede believing, and believing occurs before belonging. Several studies in UCGD support the sequence of experience to believing to belonging. Others have taken the view that church membership is initially a social experience, and faith is one dimension of social learning. Still others suggest that an individual's prior beliefs provide a kind of inner screen through which any experience is filtered, understood, and assimilated. For the New Believer, however, the experience seems primary.

Further, the experience is fundamentally religious. There is a point of contact between an individual and the divine reality. This experience presumes and authenticates the existence of a supernatural force: it is (a) grounded in God, (b) mediated through natural (as opposed to institutional) sources, and (c) perfected in loving relationships.

2. *Spiritual mystical faith.* Believers inside and outside the church share the affirmation of a divine reality. God may be seen as a transcendent power that holds the universe together or as a mystical presence who is known personally in prayer. God may take the face of Buddha or may be known in the flicker of a meditation candle or may be seen in the body of Christ on the cross. God is "out there," and the believer feels touched by that supernatural reality.

Many believers who do not belong to churches have often been bolder with their affirmations of a spiritual experience. While the pulpit still dueled against the corrosive effects of scientific methodology and logical reductionism, New Believers quietly explored the spiritual experience that had come upon them. The old battle between science and religion seems past, and the New Believers cannot remember the lines of conflict or the champions of either side. When a person is touched by a mystical experience, then the "sacred" is inseparable from the "secular." The spiritual experience has a way of synthesizing a creating, providential God with the productivity this generation takes for granted.

New Believers often have a flexibility in their faith that makes a mockery of old formulas. They can twist intellectual doubts and skepticism into an ally of faith, for "what else is there to believe in?" The traditional forms of forgiveness provide the old believer with a freedom *from sin.* But the New Believer has often suspended the rules, so that faith seems to offer a freedom *to sin,* in pursuit of the highest goal: personal religious experience. Traditionally, God is transcendent and humanity is present, but the New Believer explores the opposite experience, where God is really present and humans are the transcendent beings. As one believer explained at a late night party, "God is here, Man, and I am everywhere. It's a trip!"

Frequently, the experience of faith is so real to the New Believer that churches seem irrelevant and sometimes hypocritical. Once I saw a larger-than-life representation of Jesus Christ, a figure of compassion and physical energy, in the apartment of a New Believer. "Because of him," the believer explained, "I could never join a church. He is so real and churches are so phony."

From the base of personal religious experience with the divine, the New Believer feels qualified (even called) to reject anything less, whether it is the inadequacy of godless humanism or the emptiness of Christian rituals. I hear echoes of a prophetic voice challenging scientific process, which claims too much, and church pageantry, which believes too little.

3. *Noninstitutional sources.* Believers who do not belong have a strong inclination toward skepticism. Their faith may be positive, but the sources for that faith are often notably negative. The New Believer came into prominence with the rise of the politically independent voter (because neither party is trusted). Typically, young New Believers reject authority at all

14

levels—the draft, the job, the sergeant, parents, and, of course, the church. Their faith was born in skepticism and nourished in doubt. The sources of faith must be beyond the systems and institutions that have let them down.

Many New Believers, old and young alike, have a unique affinity with the natural world. Conservation becomes part of their faith, and ecology becomes a common cause. Others turn toward Eastern religions or other spiritual exercises to provide a quiet discipline with which to avoid the pressures of the materialistic world. Ronald Inglehart (see UCGD, chap. 4) has noted that many of the new generation have come from backgrounds in which their material needs were well cared for. They can afford to turn their attention to the development of the quality of life and to their participation in that life. Whether these changes are the result of temporary or permanent conditions is unclear. But for the moment many New Believers enjoy a Post-Materialist perspective.

The themes of faith for New Believers are ancient and are embedded in the Old and the New Testaments: mystical ties with the Creator, human affinity with the land, doubt in established authority, and a quest for quality rather than quantity of life. In support of the civil religion, the believer who does not belong can affirm the nation, without being easily entangled in political causes, or arbitrarily supporting national policies abroad. They have borrowed a kind of oriental piety, with its individualistic disciplines of withdrawal from the world for growth of the inner life.

4. *Community of love.* For New Believers, community is an ambition and a frustration. They confirm the need for community and seek fulfillment in the right kind of community. Studies have amassed long lists of communes, collectives, covenant societies, associations, and other creative arrangements. Such groups are often eclectic in their historical claims, syncretic in their teachings, and simplistic in their demands upon the individuals who belong. These communities of faith

have more recently included middle-class families and middle-aged and older adults, and have frequently embraced single-parent households to provide positive adult relationships for growing children and teenagers.

The group membership must not violate the first principle of faith: personal religious experience. They do not feel right about belonging to a group that deprives members of their individuality. Groups are expected to provide a way for each member to find personal fulfillment and continual growth. Groups must be based on the willing heart and continued satisfaction. The same standards are applied to marriage or to any significant, lasting relationship.

Thus, New Believers can join in civil rights movements and then leave at the end of a particular campaign, when the spirit seems gone. They can abandon their education for a time while they engage in the life-style of a counterculture commune, only to return to the mainstream of American life a few years later to resume traditional patterns. They can even return to management and executive positions, without the trauma of cross-cultural transition, as long as they feel the experience at the time.

Outsiders can condemn such apparently inconsistent behavior, calling them "summer soldiers," erratic and without conviction. But to those who have been moved to follow this course, such criticism only proves that the speaker is a cultural alien, an outsider, or what is much worse, the critic is a straight, a square, a "cube" who is square all over.

The sense of community suggests one basis of difference in the faith of those who belong and those who do not. New Believers base their faith in their own mystical religious experience. Mainline church members are more likely to lay claim to a flow of religious experience that predates their entry and which will continue long after they have gone. Mainline church members emphasize the historic quality of their faith but often communicate a personal flatness. New Believers can express the depth of their personal religious experience but often reflect an indifference to history. The differences in these two perspectives are difficult to cross, since each sees shadows where the other sees light.

## Mainline Church Dilemma

An increasing number of Americans are religious without joining churches. They share the faith of mainline churches—at least in the general areas suggested here—but they do not seem moved to join the churches from which the outlines of their faith have been drawn.

In one sense, this is a success story. If the church was viewed as an overbearing parent, then the children of faith have grown up and come of age. New Believers no longer need a father figure to tell them what to believe or how to pray. Their faith has found articulation, and their prayers are now their own. They seem to have absorbed many teachings of the church. They live by their understanding of Christian morality. Insofar as positive values permeate our society, the mainline churches should feel that their historic contributions have been well spent.

However, such a discovery is little comfort to those members who want to fill the sanctuary, or to pastors who want to share more openly in ministry, or to church members who feel that belonging is essential to salvation, or (not the least) to church treasurers who struggle to balance books and pay the bills. Unfortunately, the separation of believing from belonging has happened more frequently in that segment of the population from which mainline churches formerly have drawn their membership. This is clearly a national shift in values, but the institutions most affected are the mainline churches.

What did these historic churches contribute to this shift in values? Why us? Why now? And what should we do in response to these changes?

17

# CHAPTER 2

# *Portable, Affordable Religion*

That mainline churches suffer most from membership decline is no accident. The causes of declining statistics are built in the values of the churches and the priorities of their members. God, working through events of history, might have provided another way. But all other things being as they were, the mainline churches could not have prevented these events, even if they had been able to foresee these changes. Their contributions to membership loss appear to be the natural, unconscious working out of the Christian virtues that they proclaimed and the American Dream which their members pursued. Mainline churches contributed to these declining statistics simply by being true to themselves.

## The American Dream

Beyond the baseline beliefs that they hold in common with believers who do not belong, mainline Protestant congregations have been leading proponents of the American Dream. So clearly and frequently has the affirmation of faith and the ambition of people been joined that many church members cannot easily separate Christian from American middle-class values. Every believer has a personal way of stating these priorities, and every pastor has favorite phrases that combine these basic values. Throughout the collected research, the following themes were clearly and consistently associated with church memberships:

1. *Religious belief.* In national samples, church members have widely supported several orthodox tenets of the Christian faith, including faith in God; belief in Jesus Christ as the Son of God, or as God; belief in the Bible as the word of God; practice of prayer; and expectation of life after death. Although these doctrines are strongly held among church members, we should note that these faith statements are also held by people who do not participate in churches. They are broadly supported, even by New Believers. Further, they are statements about a personal relationship between the individual and the divine being. Apparently, these faith statements do not need institutional church support and are individualized in character. These beliefs provide a faith the believer can keep in the inner life and can take within himself or herself on any kind of journey. This faith is portable.

2. *Congregational commitment.* Believers who join churches tend to emphasize the importance of social belonging in two ways. For some people, community is located in the place of belonging—my church building, my church neighborhood, my church family, my locality. Clark Roof (UCGD, chap. 2) has called attention to this concept of localism as an important factor in congregational life. Localism, when understood to embrace the stability of family patterns, the strength of community friendship networks, and the social composition of the community, has broad support in the collected research on Protestant church membership values. Conversely, social mobility and population diversity adversely affect the numerical strength of American churches.

Social status provides another expression of social belonging. In status groups a church member associates with "my sort of people." Although there is overwhelming evidence that congregations tend to be composed primarily of a single class and a single ethnicity, church members are seldom willing to identify social reasons as an important motivation in choosing a particular congregation.

Both localism and social status are important definitions of community in our Protestant heritage: localism reflects the geographic parish understanding of congregational life; similarity of social status reflects a gathered community of those who share a common calling.

3. *Nuclear family.* The American Christian lifts up the virtues of the nuclear family as an ideal goal for every believer. This elemental family unit has prevailed against the alternatives of an extended family, on the one hand, or the celibacy of the Christian calling, on the other. Parents and their offspring together make up the most important social unit for the believers who belong to American churches.

In a positive way, the emphasis upon the children of church families has created the largest single program emphasis for mainline churches—the Sunday school. Ruth T. Doyle and Sheila M. Kelly (UCGD, chap. 6) have shown that church school membership is an excellent index to predict subsequent church membership; gains or losses in church school participation in a given year will be reflected in denominational membership five years later. Although church schools have often reached out into surrounding communities, beyond the children of their own members, the emphasis upon children and youth is one positive indication of the family ties that attract and hold members in local churches. Families with school-age children are more likely to become church members than any other segment of the population.

In a negative way, mainline church members are vigorous in their reactions against any perceived threat to the nuclear family. Since abortion, divorce, homosexuality, and ERA are often seen as undermining the nuclear family, these issues are emotionally opposed by many church members. The most threatening issues that have attracted the attention of the mainline churches are not the broad political, social, and economic causes, but the more intimate challenges which imply changes in traditional sex relationships or the development of nonnuclear family life-styles.

4. *Individual fulfillment.* The importance of the individual believer is at the center of the Christian affirmations of the American Dream. The individual believer expects fulfillment through personal faith, individual responsibility, and continued growth "in the nurture and admonition of the Lord." Individual response is the target of the Protestant invitation of faith. Individual responsibility is the basis for private morality. Individual growth is the assumption that motivates believers to higher, more specialized levels of education and professional training.

The kinds of personal satisfactions that move people toward church membership have been the subject of a whole range of studies. These are usually formulated in the negative: What was missing from a person's life that church membership seems to fulfill or satisfy? With few exceptions, the results of this kind of inquiry have been frustrating. Studies have shown that many people who have personal, psychological, and spiritual needs seek out the church for assistance. There is further evidence that members of churches claim to be slightly happier than the general population. But no studies have been able to demonstrate that church membership was responsible for changing individuals from those in need to those who were happier. Perhaps we must rely on the testimony of "satisfied customers" whom we have known personally. Or, as some researchers have suggested, individuals may join congregations for reasons of personal need but continue in membership for reasons of faith and more generalized social relationships.

In summary, these four concepts consistently correlate with Protestant church membership in affirmation of the American Dream: religious belief, congregational commitment, nuclear family, and individual fulfillment. If they had been held of equal value, the numerical strength of the mainline churches might have gone unchanged. Unfortunately, the members of mainline churches apparently have prioritized these values in a way that made the loss of church members inevitable. They have believed too much in some and not enough in others. Examples of these shifts in emphasis can be seen in three areas: the suburban migration of members, the general mobility of the middle class, and the declining church participation in those denominations that most affirmed the American middle-class Dream.

## Suburban Strategy

"At least we still have the suburbs," consoled one church executive. "This is basically a suburban society, and we have our strength in the suburbs."

Following World War II the suburban expansion of the cities seemed to offer both the soil and the need for fertile church growth. Mainline church membership soared where the elements were right; namely, Protestant families who were younger, aggressive, affluent, new to the community, and above all, parents of school-age children. Church families abandoned the problems of the city in search of fulfillment for themselves and their children in suburbia. The organization of suburban congregations consumed much of the undesignated income for mainline Protestant churches from 1950 through the mid-1960s. Churches scrambled to keep up with the opportunities for new congregations serving developing subdivisions.

Suburban living seemed tailored to the values of the American Dream. Great pastures were cut into green patches for private dwellings to house nuclear families (built without space for mothers-in-law), constructed in communities that were designed to appeal to a specific level of income and taste. Economic homogeneity was built into the community design.

Racial and sometimes even ethnic homogeneity was assumed by the real estate industry, enforced by the banking industry, and sanctioned by the administration of veterans' funds and FHA mortgages. The suburbs seemed to assure communities of "our kind of people." White mainline churches from the city often moved to suburban communities or junctions of arterial highways to be close to "our people."

At the same time, mainline churches fared poorly in changing urban neighborhoods. Congregations that were once strong anchors of city communities watched as their members moved to the green pastures and the quiet politics of the suburbs. The problems of the diversified city parish were traded for the promise of new suburban living. As city churches became alienated from their neighborhoods, membership declined. Without clear-cut policies, denominations sometimes subsidized declining urban congregations and sometimes allowed them to drift into dissolution. For the most part, denominations did not provide the necessary resources for those congregations that were racially mixed, economically depressed, or ministering in highly congested, older areas of the cities. The price was too high in the city, and the opportunities were too great in the suburbs.

"What the cities have lost the suburbs have gained—at least in the way of church members," suggests Douglas A. Walrath (UCGD, chap. 11), paraphrasing an attitude widely held by white mainline churches. Although embarrassed by their inability to attract new members from different cultural groups in the city, mainline churches consoled themselves by the exchange. What they had lost in the cities, they hoped to win back in the suburbs.

They failed. In this move, mainline churches were forced to admit that their form of the gospel was not universal. In practical fact, mainline denominations acknowledged that their expression of the faith was limited to a particular class and often to a particular ethnic group. The gospel as they knew it, sang it, prayed it, and preached it had developed a flavor that was distinctively middle class and usually Wasp.

The social, economic, and cultural homogeneity of congregations in particular and denominations in general is treated quite differently throughout UCGD. As social scientists, most of the authors take note of the correlations and seek to untangle the elements that make the relationships so strong. From a historical and a theological viewpoint, several authors accept the guilt burden, articulated by Gibson Winter, that the mainline churches are the captives of the suburban culture which they did so much to create (see UCGD, chaps. 3 and 13). By contrast, the vigorous, new Institute for Church Growth, inspired by Donald McGavran, at Fuller Theological Seminary, has collected data on the conditions under which certain populations are more or less receptive to their presentation of the gospel. For church growth analysts, like C. Peter Wagner (UCGD, chap. 12), the homogeneous unit recognizes the medium of homogeneous populations through which the gospel is most effectively communicated. For Wagner, homogeneity is not an embarrassment but a practical process through which the power of God can flow.

For mainline denominations that preach the universality of the American Christian dream, the cultural limitations of homogeneity were seen as more than an embarrassment: it was a devastating discovery. To compensate, urban congregations and minority causes were elevated for special attention in denominational media. Several national denominations supported legislation that would assure all Americans of their civil rights and would remove the blight of poverty from "the richest nation on earth." These twin crusades were designed to offer the American Dream to every citizen. Unfortunately, they were distracted by a war in Vietnam and then were buried in a tide of doubt and cynicism.

The self-criticism of mainline denominations degenerated into what James H. Smylie (UCGD, chap. 3) has called the era of Wasp-swatting. Mainline churches lost confidence in their priorities, their policies, and most of all, their theological purity. They lost a compelling image of the future. Suburban living was no longer an adequate American dream.

## *Mobility as a Mind-set*

Middle-class mobility did not stop with a move to the suburbs. The American Dream that motivated the construction of the first suburban communities later supported the development of another, bigger and better. The new suburbs promised more private space to raise a family among the right kind of people, more recreational space, more amenities, more social status, for those families who had really made it! The promises that made the suburbs kept them moving.

Mobility of the nuclear family became, for some occupations, a measure of success. Some families moved to communities more appropriate to their new economic standing; their affluence provided the financial resources to pay for better housing. Others moved when they found new employment in other communities, or when their present employers had need for them to be assigned to the same industry in another city, just one step up the ladder of success.

The nuclear family is a remarkably mobile social unit. It can be stripped of all sentimental restraints due to overattachment to significant places or to family and close personal friends. For the sake of the nuclear family, and especially "for the children," the urgency of higher income and better employment can seem like a divine imperative to the middle-class Christian who is possessed by the American Dream. Community—even the most idyllic of suburban estates—is sacrificed for yet another move when the right opportunity comes along. Americans move more often than any other "settled" people in history. Those who remain must adjust to the fluidity of others in their midst. Mobility becomes a state of mind.

25

The cultural socialization of children and of youth prepares them for their years as mobile adults. At home children are urged to think for themselves, to make decisions, to live in their own space, to be responsible for their personal possessions. In higher education children are often permitted or encouraged to leave home, to separate from the oversight of family and the fabric of community life. Friends made in college are scattered as each chooses a location based on employment opportunities. In their new communities the recent arrivals lack the base of shared personal experiences and the histories of common family backgrounds. Whatever beliefs and values they may have, have been brought with them. Faith is a personal and usually a private experience. Community is a temporary arrangement.

Localism—the sense of belonging among a people in a place—bears a strong positive correlation with church membership. Churches tend to draw members from those people who share family ties and friendship networks, who are similar in cultural heritage and in personal life-styles, who hold values in common and who support one another in the values they share. Clark Roof suggests that these plausibility structures provide an important function of mutual support for church members. Unfortunately, the localism upon which many congregations depend is measurably reduced by mobility, in general, and by higher education, in particular. The values of nuclear family and of personal fulfillment have provided the rationale for ever-increasing mobility. Both social and economic mobility have directly contributed to the decline of the congregational life in which they are spawned.

Changing communities, social mobility, and alienated populations are the enemies of congregational strength in neighborhood churches. Douglas Walrath (UCGD, chap. 11) offers graphic support to show the effects upon church membership as social mobility touches different neighborhoods in a city in upstate New York. The inner urban church membership was declining before 1950, while churches in the outer urban

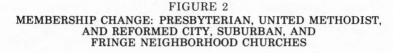

FIGURE 2
MEMBERSHIP CHANGE: PRESBYTERIAN, UNITED METHODIST,
AND REFORMED CITY, SUBURBAN, AND
FRINGE NEIGHBORHOOD CHURCHES

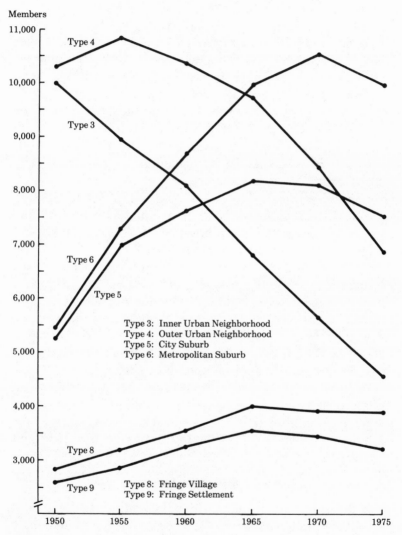

27

areas showed membership losses in the early 1950s. Congregations located in older suburban communities (city suburbs) grew more slowly and declined more gently. New suburban congregations (in metropolitan suburbs) grew more rapidly and peaked more decisively, about 1970. No neighborhood congregation was immune from change. The mobility that created suburban congregations eventually came full cycle to threaten each new layer of metropolitan growth.

Parenthetically, Roman Catholic church members show their commitment to the American Dream in patterns of church participation that more nearly approximate Protestant congregations every year. Through the mid-1960s the Catholic statistics on membership participation were sustained by classic examples of plausibility structures in ethnoreligious communities in which faith was shared and values were overtly enforced. In the suburban migration of middle-class Catholics and in the urban transition of older ethnic communities the plausibility structures have deteriorated. At the same time, Catholic parishes in suburban areas are much more likely to be voluntary communities of highly mobile nuclear families. In the past decade the worship participation of Catholics, in a typical week, has declined from 71 percent to 54 percent. Among younger Catholics the percentage of worship participation is becoming indistinguishable from the behavior of their Protestant neighbors (less than 40 percent).

In pursuit of the Christian American Dream, both Catholic and Protestant church members have placed a premium on individual fulfillment and the nuclear family. Consequently, community strength and the quality of congregational life have suffered.

### *Affordable Faith*

A third demonstration of the paralyzing commitments of mainline church members to the values of the American Dream can be seen in the responses of the churches to the crisis of declining membership statistics. Denominational leaders were under pressure to find the causes for membership decline and to develop an appropriate denominational response. The most widely quoted analysis and advocacy was articulated by Dean M. Kelley, a Methodist, who serves on the staff of the National Council of Churches. In his book *Why Conservative Churches Are Growing,* Kelley urges membership loyalty for the sake of congregational solidarity: Church discipline is more pertinent than individual beliefs; missionary zeal is more necessary than social action; and a distinctive community style is more important than individual life-style for each member. Many denominational leaders have supported his call for loyalty, solidarity, zeal, distinctiveness, and above all, discipline.

Because of the importance and the wide acceptance of these recommendations, many of the studies included and cited in UCGD contain information designed to test their effectiveness. In particular, Dean Hoge (UCGD, chap. 8) reviewed the literature and attempted to ascertain the correlations between the Kelley thesis and membership growth or decline in sixteen denominations. The relationships he found between church membership and loyalty, solidarity, zeal, distinctiveness, and discipline were all in the anticipated direction and were strongly positive. The Kelley thesis appeared to provide the characteristics of theology and program that distinguished between growing and declining denominations. On the surface, the results seemed to offer the appropriate analysis and the recommended programmatic response. Some denominational leaders rushed to the podium with recommendations for denominational programs calling for loyalty, solidarity, zeal, distinctiveness, and discipline. Such programs were enacted by church judicatories. Unfortunately, these calls for more vigorous action were generally ignored by congregations. Kelley's disciplined approach was unenforceable rhetoric for the middle-class members of mainline Protestant churches. Chapter 4 examines the Kelley thesis more thoroughly and explores the policies and programs consistent with mainline church membership growth.

Hoge's study of the Kelley thesis is especially significant for this chapter because it underscores the preexisting class values that seem to determine which programs are effective with particular denominations. Although it is true, as noted above, that the Kelley principles correlated positively with growing denominations and negatively with declining denominations, Hoge added two more factors: The higher socioeconomic status of the denomination (rated in family income) provided a negative correlation with growth, accounting for more than half the variance between growing and declining denominations. Although program decisions undoubtedly had some effect upon the social groups attracted to the church, it must be assumed that economic status factors of the population preceded the program decisions. Further, Hoge found that the more a denomination affirmed the American life-style, the more it suffered from declining membership. In the period 1965-75 the correlation between affirmation of the American life-style and church growth was −.97! Faith in the American Dream had a direct negative effect upon the membership of mainline churches.

In summary, mainline Wasp religion and the American Dream have a common base in the Christian faith, in congregational commitments, in the nuclear family, and in individual fulfillment. Chapter 1 notes that the first of these, faith, has been privatized, apparently without need for continuing institutional support. An increasing number of people believe without belonging. For them, the church has become optional equipment.

This chapter discusses the erosion of the community as reflected in the mobility of the American middle class. Initially, upward mobility to suburban communities contributed to the growth of church membership statistics in the 1950s. This form of church growth largely depended on developing new con-

## FIGURE 3
## PLOT OF FAMILY INCOME BY GROWTH 1965-1975

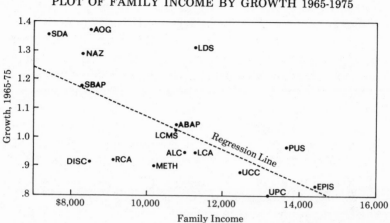

## FIGURE 4
## PLOT OF DISTINCTIVE LIFE-STYLE BY GROWTH 1965-1975

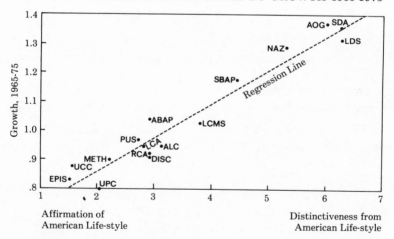

ABAP=American Baptist; ALC=American Lutheran Ch.; AOG=Assemblies of God; DISC=Disciples of Christ; EPIS=Episcopal; LCA=Lutheran Ch. in America; LCMS=Lutheran Ch.-Missouri Synod; LDS=Latter Day Saints; METH=Methodist; NAZ=Church of the Nazarene; PUS=Presbyterian, U.S.; RCA=Reformed Church in Am.; SBAP=Southern Baptist; SDA=Seventh Day Adventist; UCC=United Church of Christ; UPC=United Presbyterian

31

gregations from homogeneous populations. Continued mobility, which at first made possible the strength of suburban congregations, eventually undermined the community continuities of faith and shared experience upon which congregational life is constructed. In the past decade many mainline churches in suburban communities have become as vulnerable to transient populations as city churches were a decade or two earlier.

Of the Christian-American Dream, two points are notable: Faith has been privatized, and congregational life has been undermined. Little wonder that those denominations which embraced the American Dream most clearly subsequently have suffered the sharpest decline in church membership. The two remaining values—nuclear family and individual fulfillment—provide the themes for the next chapter.

# CHAPTER 3

# *Where Have All Our People Gone?*

Mainline church members have not literally gotten up from their pews on Sunday and walked out, never to return. The amazing fact is that most families who relocate join other congregations. The new church, often in another denomination, is more convenient, more prepared with needed services, or more appropriate to the family's status in the new community. Given the erosive effect that mobility has upon community, membership statistics have remained remarkably stable; they could be much worse.

Mainline church membership losses are not the result of an increase in the number of persons who have dropped out of congregations, but rather the opposite: a decreasing number of people have joined the churches and thus do not compensate for the normal attrition. Mainline church members are getting older. The median age creeps up as older members are not matched by an influx of young blood. The primary (although not the only) cause of membership decline is the churches' inability to attract and hold young members. Such causality is true, but as with the politician who explained why he failed to be elected by saying that he did not get enough votes, more needs to be said.

## *Family Life Cycle*

One approach to the absence of youth in our congregations is a straightforward analysis of the age structure of the

33

population. Currently, we are in a trough between the wave of young parents who passed through society in the 1950s and the next wave of young parents, who will enter society in the mid-1980s. One school of thought, carefully articulated by Widick Schroeder, offers generally optimistic advice: When the elements are right, the people will return to those congregations where they felt welcome. The "votes" are there, when all the returns are in.

The optimistic prognosis is based on a theory of church membership which is so simple that many pastors have taken it for granted. In essence, it assumes that people with middle-class values and ambitions pass through a family life cycle in which the church is particularly important at different phases of the journey. For young adults, religious participation is anticipated to be relatively low, since their energies are directed toward establishing a career and beginning a family. During the middle years, parents of school-age children are supposed to be more active in church, primarily to ensure the religious education of their children. Religious participation is expected to decline in later years, when the children mature and the nest is empty and older adults may turn to other interests. According to this approach, when the present young adults reach the stage of parenting school-age children, they will return as a family.

Because supporting research would greatly relieve the anxiety of mainline church leadership, the family cycle thesis has been examined from a variety of perspectives. Three elements uphold this comforting scenario. First, consistently, young adults in their 20s participate in church less frequently than other age groups. Prior to parenting, they seem to be engaged in many pursuits outside the church, from studying in preparation for careers to the sowing of wild oats. The first phase of the pattern is widely supported. The second phase receives a mixed review: School-age children in the home do make the family more receptive to invitations toward church membership; they seem at least to contribute to the inclination to belong. However, infants and teenagers in the home do not appear to make much difference or perhaps contribute in a negative way. Finally, postparenting adults are inclined to become more active and increase their church participation when the nest is empty—an unpredicted but pleasant surprise. It is this final factor that helps to explain why mainline churches are statistically older and more affluent than the general population.

If all these projected statistical trends could just be held in place, we could close the books on church membership decline and could look for building contractors to begin to expand the present facilities.

## *Values in Conflict*

Unfortunately, this description does not include all the essential information. We speculated on straight-line projections in the church building boom of the early 1960s; that error should not be repeated. Assurance is needed that young adults will follow the traditional family life cycle patterns on which those projections are based. If values have changed, as has been suggested, what reason have we to believe that our children will follow in our footsteps?

First, the statistical support for the family life cycle pattern is inconsistent and unpredictable. As each age group passes through the life cycle, significant current events prove to be equally important as their life stage in determining church participation. The events of the late 1960s and the early 1970s have made such an impression on the youth that we must be concerned about any simple predictions regarding future church attendance.

Second, the shift in youth participation in the church is more clearly defined than it has been in the past. David Roozen has called this separation of the age groups a polarization of social attitudes. The distance between the older generation and the young adults is growing with every survey. Whatever is affecting church participation in general has been felt more sharply among youth, or at least they were able to respond more easily.

But youth are not the only age group to decline in church participation. The percentage of weekly church participation by young families and postparenting adults has also fallen, although not as dramatically. Older adults have remained members of mainline churches and apparently have increased their financial support. In fact, the church participation of older adults, in many congregations, may have postponed the sense of urgency to find younger members. Such a delay may pose an even greater crisis in mainline churches within the next decade. Participation is declining in all three age groups, but losses are most dramatic among the young.

FIGURE 5
WEEKLY CHURCH ATTENDANCE WITHIN
THREE AGE GROUPS

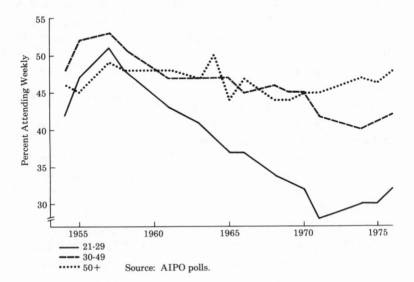

——— 21-29
— — 30-49
•••••• 50+          Source: AIPO polls.

Third, and most devastating, the values challenged by the youth are fixed on the areas where middle-class church members appear to be most sensitive. Based on studies included and cited in UCGD, the polarities between older adults who belong to churches and younger adults who are less likely to belong can be dramatized:

| Attitudes of Church Members and Older Adults | Attitudes of Younger Adults and Fewer Church Members |
| --- | --- |
| Faith: orthodox doctrine | Faith: personal experience |
| Belong to church and accept its traditions | Question all authority and doubt institutional promises |
| Localism: | Cosmopolitanism: |
|    family high priority |    individual high priority |
|    larger families |    less interested in children |
|    ethnic and community ties |    cultural diversity |
|    happier |    restless |
| Emphasis on community moral standards | Emphasis on individual decision about personal life-styles |
| Economic free enterprise | Advocacy for individual freedoms |
| Fear of Communism | Independent politics, political pluralism |
| Greater opposition to | Greater acceptance of |
|    premarital sex |    premarital sex |
|    extramarital sex |    extramarital sex |
|    abortion |    abortion |
|    divorce |    divorce |
|    homosexuality |    homosexuality |
|    pornography |    pornography |
|    birth control (RC)* |    birth control (RC)* |
|    remarriage (RC)* |    remarriage (RC)* |

*Applies primarily to Roman Catholics.

The difference in these perspectives cannot be explained simply by age differentials. Young adults who have experienced college and higher education are far more likely to share the values of the generational unit to which they belong. Young adults who have not finished high school are more likely to share the values of their parents and their community. Thus, there are different perspectives among the young adults as a single age group.

The chart showing white Protestant church attendance has two implications for American churches. On the one hand, it should be a comfort to those denominations and congregations that draw members from portions of the population which are relatively free from shifts in values and in cultural perspectives that are associated with a college education. While

FIGURE 6
WHITE PROTESTANT CHURCH ATTENDANCE
BY EDUCATION, 1952-1968

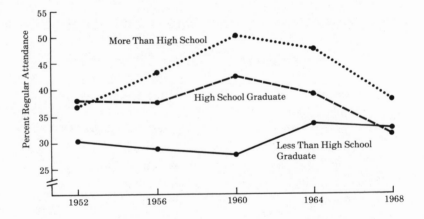

other groups have declined in support from young adults, churches drawing from lower socioeconomic sectors of the population have gained. If the trends of this chart continued after 1968, it would account for some of the growth in the nonmainline churches during the past decade. Such a conclusion would find firm support in the positive correlations between church growth and lower family incomes and between church decline and affirmation of the American life-style, as reported in chapter 2.

On the other hand, this chart suggests that there is little relief in sight for mainline denominations. This conflict in values is most frequently found in that section of the population from which mainline churches have traditionally drawn their strength. More than likely the youth who espouse these new values come from families that have higher incomes, higher levels of education, and greater social mobility. They have been taught to think for themselves and have learned to put a premium on their personal experiences. As Post-Materialists, they have not had to worry about the physical necessities of life and have been free to concentrate on the quality of life. The higher their level of educational attainment, the more young people will belong to their generational unit and will espouse the values in conflict listed above.

These young people represent the "lost members" of mainline churches. They are the children of our homes, in previous generations the largest source of membership. They may yet return and refill the empty pews. Many have joined mainline churches; some have joined other congregations. Most have joined nothing, and yet they keep the faith.

### Young Believers

For the sake of dialogue, let us note several characteristics of Young Believers as contrasted with the values of an older generation.

Young Believers are not secularists; at least not in the traditional sense. They carry many of the values of the New Believers described in chapter 1. They believe strongly in a divine being, as known through their own mystical experience, without any necessity for the intervention of the institutional church. They are more than humanists or rationalists; they believe in God, Jesus, prayer, and life beyond death.

As Post-Materialists, they travel light. Their faith is portable, and their confidence is rooted in their own experience. They expect to find their satisfactions as they travel, with their companions on the trip. They have shed the extended family (with the complications of aunts and uncles, cousins and in-laws) and invest their emotional energy in spouses, careers, and offspring. They have discarded the family heirlooms and find identity in their chosen standard of living. They are more apt to collect classical music than sentimental furniture.

Sometimes they travel even lighter. More young families are having fewer children or none at all. More young families are retooling their marriage relationships or are breaking up and starting over. More young adults are changing their jobs or careers or life-styles. They need a faith that can keep up with their changes.

Young Believers are not irresponsible in the tasks they accept. There is no widespread protest from employers that these young adults perform poorly or fail to show up on the job. Contracts and agreements are honored for the time being, not forever. Nothing is forever. They contract for their services, but they live self-contained lives. They are not irresponsible, but they expect each person to be responsible for him or herself. Life-style is a personal choice. Morality is a private decision.

Therefore, they are tolerant and even accepting of many activities that traditional society has viewed as threatening and that the church has condemned. Older church members often view the Young Believer as a kind of happy hedonist, seeking only the satisfactions of the inflated self. The Young Believer often views the church members as rigid dogmatists who have not experienced life or the spirit. Many values that youth have emphasized are those principles on which church members have found compromise most difficult. The conflict is most sensitive and emotional with regard to home and family values and the sexual mores that support or threaten the stability of the "Christian" (nuclear) American family. As Robert Wuthnow has acknowledged (see UCGD, chap. 4), the number of young people who openly advocate these values may be a minority, but the effect seems to permeate the larger generational unit.

Consistent with the faith of the New Believers, the younger generation has evolved a distinct style for reaching decisions. They are far more inclined to separate private behavior from public morality. They are more tolerant of life-styles with which they do not agree, of political parties that might threaten the established order, of disruptive ideas and disturbing literature. They are far more apt to challenge the claims of institutional authority or the decisions of majority rule, if these intrude upon individual liberties or personal freedom.

For Young Believers, the emphasis rests upon an inner satisfaction rather than logical certainty or social acceptance. They do not seek social sanctions or institutional authorization for their actions or feelings. They do not trust the institutional systems to deliver in any field—political, social, economic, military, or spiritual. Therefore, they have few inhibitions about multiple associations with vastly different groups, such as remaining a Methodist while practicing the Zen Buddhist religious disciplines. Labels are not important; it's the heart that counts.

In that spirit, the youth culture sees no need for church membership: values are in conflict. Decisions rest on different premises and are made with different priorities. Institutions have a poor track record for delivery on promises. Other associations may prove more productive in the search for a more satisfying quality of life.

With values so different and attitudes so fixed, it sometimes appears that the church and youth are on parallel tracks, each headed for infinity. But they are on such different courses, with a constant distance between them that is not easily bridged. Why bother trying to close the gap? Two reasons: First, the absence of these young people is the cause of declining church membership. They are the traditional source of new members for mainline denominations. Second, they are still "our people." After discussing these values, an elderly couple said, "Thank you for explaining our children to us. They are good kids, living in (another city). But church just doesn't mean the same thing to them that it does to us." A young pastor responded, "They may be your kids, but they are my best friends from college and from here in the neighborhood." They are still our people, and we cannot easily let them go.

Our people did not leave the mainline churches in anger or in apathy. They were carried away by a shift in cultural values, to which the church has made a major contribution. But they have not gone anywhere. For most mainline churches, the previous sources of membership are still in the community and are not even alienated from our congregations. They are the children of our elders and the best friends of our pastors, and yet they are unmoved toward church membership. They are the young New Believers.

# Part Two

# CHAPTER 4

# *Choices for Churches*

In this decade of declining membership, mainline churches have experienced the chill of self-doubt. Just when it seemed as though the religious boom of the '50s would last forever, somebody changed the rules of the game. The oldest and most prestigious denominations suffered the largest losses. For mainline denominations, this membership decline is the most serious and sustained reversal of religious trends since the founding of the nation. In losing members, the established churches began to lose self-confidence.

In their tradition of prophetic judgment, these mainline churches were no less critical of themselves than they were of the larger social order: "We have seen the enemy, and they is us," confessed Pogo, for a generation of contrite and confused Christians. These churches made confession, even for sins they did not commit, but they were not reborn with vitality for membership growth. Mainline churches experienced a serious failure of nerve. They doubted themselves.

Institutionally, these denominations reorganized for a new start. Theologically, religious thinkers offered a whole smorgasbord of attractive new images to nourish the church back to life. These denominations ventured out in search of dramatic new ministries, from new-style congregations to far-out social causes. At the same time, their world mission was shrinking, and the development of new congregations in the United States almost ceased.

Mainline churches appear to be surrounded by potential membership populations. Much of the information that correlates with church growth does not lend itself to easy program development in search of new members. Family size affects church membership, but we know of no denomination that is encouraging a higher birthrate for the purpose of reversing membership trends. Regionalism affects church participation, since people in the southern states attend church more frequently than in other sections of the country. Yet, we have not heard of congregations moving south so that they might enjoy more responsive popular support, in the way that some business enterprises move south for cheap labor. A particular socioeconomic status is frequently associated with specific denominations, but we have not seen a denominational strategy to change its socioeconomic status for the purpose of more rapid growth. We can identify factors that affect church growth and decline, but many of these are beyond the reach of human decisions. Within these limits, denominational strategy and local congregational efforts can make a difference.

What mainline churches lack, according to several contributors to UCGD, is an identity of purpose, a clarity of task, a compelling image that arouses believers to action, in the name of the Lord. Mainline churches have a sense of urgency and a wide choice of images. But which is the appropriate stance for these churches at this particular time and place?

## Three Choices

Sociological analyses can provide essential information and can raise important issues based on the perceptions of many people. But only faith can point the way to a compelling image for the mainline churches at this time. Whatever the choice, we should not ignore those persons who once supported mainline denominations. Yet, how can religious institutions appeal to people who believe but have no apparent need for belonging?

How can the church provide a sense of community for those who have developed a mobile mind-set and life-style? How can churches bridge the conflict of values to the young believers, without losing the support of the old? Given the trends of religion in America, is there a way for mainline denominations to rekindle relationships with the populations from which they once drew their support?

Three approaches have been urged upon the churches with such compelling force that they have gathered widespread support and frequently find their way into denominational and congregational studies. The first approach advocates a clear, disciplined theological distinction between Christians in the churches and the world outside. This position has been stated with winsome power in the watershed work of Dean M. Kelley, *Why Conservative Churches Are Growing.* A second way is based on the missiological studies of the Church Growth Institute, which uses tools of social analysis to discern the receptivity of a population toward the gospel. This approach has been forcefully stated by C. Peter Wagner in *Your Church Can Grow.* The third way is the historic emphasis of the Reformation churches, which have accepted responsibility for the care of individual souls and for the welfare of the society as a whole. Martin Marty, in *The Righteous Empire: The Protestant Experience in America,* has noted the public function of mainline churches of mediating significant values in the general culture. Since each of these authors is included in UCGD and each of these themes was widely discussed and frequently measured, we shall consider them as symbolic of the available choices.

### Strong Christian Churches

Dean Kelley begins with an affirmation of strong Christian churches that stand apart from the evils of the world. He urges Christians toward a church that is distinctively "Christian" in

47

its belief and in its behavior. Persons need to sacrifice to join the strong Christian church, and they must be willing to suffer discipline in order to remain members. With such group solidarity, members will be marked by missionary zeal to tell the good news with winsomeness, warmth, and confidence. The marks of the church will be institutional strictness, separation from the world, theological conservatism, and an urgency to invite others to forsake the world and join them.

Dean Kelley presented his thesis with simplicity and sincerity in 1972, when concerned church leaders were looking for an explanation. His statistics were devastating and his theology was appealing. Kelley argued that mainline denominations were declining in membership because they were too weak to adhere to the marks of the church: institutional strictness, worldly separation, theological conservatism, and evangelical zeal. He pointed enthusiastically to the denominations that were growing, suggesting that they had maintained the necessary strength of Christian commitment.

Fortunately, the same clarity that makes the Kelley thesis appealing also makes it possible for the impact of his approach to be tested in large denominations and in particular congregations. Does the absence of Kelley's marks of the church correlate with declining churches, and does the presence of these characteristics correlate with growing congregations? If these components correlated, then can we say they cause growth or decline? If they cause membership changes, then can we convince the congregations that these elements should be instituted? Church researchers took up the challenge. No recent thesis has been given so much attention in the development of research instruments in mainline denominations.

Two national studies of congregations (UCGD, chaps. 9 and 10) considered elements of the Kelley thesis as expressed in growing and declining congregations. The United Presbyterians found measurements for the marks of the church—strictness, separation, conservatism, and zeal. The

United Church of Christ study developed a scale for theological liberalism/conservatism and several measures for intensity of membership involvement. In both studies conservatism was measured by emphasis, not absolute differences. Conservatives emphasized personal religious experience for salvation, personal faith in daily decisions, the authority of the Bible as the ("infallible") word of God, and a concern for life after death. Both denominations were interested in testing the effectiveness of the Kelley thesis in their congregations. The conclusion was the same for both: the presence or absence of the Kelley marks of the church did not correlate with growing mainline congregations. Several other studies that compared a cross section of congregations reached similar conclusions.

Under the most careful examination of congregational traits in mainline denominations, the characteristics of strength defined by Kelley are no more likely to be found in growing mainline churches than in declining ones. Social contextual factors apparently beyond the control of the local congregation seem to predetermine the potential limits for growth. Nevertheless, Dean Kelley (UCGD, chap. 15) urges the churches to renew their resolve and to keep on trying.

The Kelley thesis is complicated by personal experience. We all know of numerous situations in which the disciplines he urges are dramatically effective. We may know of congregations of equally committed Christians who continue to decline in membership, even as they grow in spiritual depth and discipleship; for them the Kelley thesis failed to produce more members. We know of churches that simply failed to try.

The Kelley thesis does not work as a universal solution—which is the way it is first presented. But it does prove effective for specific churches in particular situations. In both the United Church of Christ and the United Presbyterian Church studies, growing congregations in settled, metropolitan communities exhibited many of the characteristics Kelley reported. Specifically, in older city and in nongrowing suburban communities the growing churches clearly distinguished themselves from the community, made higher demands upon the members, expected members to recruit others, and spent more time sharing their conservative faith. To the degree that metropolitan communities were defined as nongrowing, congregations seemed to relate effectiveness with higher levels of commitment and discipline. They had institutional strictness, worldly separation, theological conservatism, and evangelical zeal, just as Kelley predicted.

But these congregations had more, and much of the rest of their program and beliefs contradicted the typical definition of conservative churches. In settled suburbs and cities the growing congregations were distinctive from but involved in the life of their communities; they were conservative, but they also organized for the disadvantaged; they actively recruited members, but they also advocated for social justice. These energetic congregations were capable of doing it all—and they did it with enthusiasm. The discipline and commitment of the Kelley thesis is effective, but not everywhere and not with the social limitations that conservative spokespersons have often implied. For congregations in settled metropolitan areas, Kelley offers a useful model for local churches.

Dean Kelley's thesis did appear to have the support of twenty-one expert observers, who rated the policies and programs of sixteen denominations. Based on their independent but highly corroborative ratings, denominations with characteristics anticipated by Kelley were found to be the denominations with the highest rates of membership increase.

However, when seeking to determine if these Kelley characteristics were causes of growth or simply correlations from a third source, Dean Hoge (as discussed earlier in chapter 2) correlated socioeconomic variables with denominational growth and decline. He found that contextual factors—socioeconomic status and region—accounted for more than half of the denominational growth in the past decade. The higher the socioeconomic status, the greater the membership losses. Hoge suggested that the Kelley characteristics are important in those social settings which involve some separateness from mainline culture and from main power structures. Conversely, the Kelley thesis was found to be ineffective among people who are wealthy or cosmopolitan in their social values.

From this research it seems that the Kelley thesis has a firm basis in at least one segment of the society, with both socioeconomic and theological implications. Socially, it appears to have the greatest impact among people who already feel alienated economically, politically, educationally, psychologically, and spiritually. Thus, the Kelley thesis has a strong kinship with the many evangelistic efforts that have spoken to the physical, social, and spiritual deprivations which have moved many people to seek the spiritual guidance of the church. Churches with an emphasis upon social action or suburban socialization have often overlooked these pressing personal needs. Theologically, it appears that people with such feelings of deprivation may express their faith in more specific terms: disciplined communities, separate from an "evil" culture; personal morality more than social ethics; and reassurance that they have found the One Way.

Although the Kelley thesis may not explain why most mainline denominations are declining in membership, the absence of any Kelley characteristics in many congregations may be a further indication of the cultural elitism of mainline Protestant churches and of their insensitivity to personal need and community crisis. Selective use of the Kelley thesis can play an important role in the renewal of congregations and denominations.

Unfortunately, for our use of this work, Dean Kelley does not make the classical distinction between church and sect. Historically, mainline churches have been the carriers of Christian cultural values: devotion to God, fidelity to family, honesty in industry, and integrity in public affairs. In these ways the establishment churches have proudly contributed to the growth of the stronger nation. In the classic sense, they are churches. The marks of the church that Kelley applies have more traditionally been applied to sectarian religion, which is over against the culture: institutional strictness, worldly separation, theological conservatism, and evangelical zeal. The examples he cites (UCGD, chap. 15) are clearly sectarian: Assemblies of God, Jehovah's Witnesses, Seventh-Day Adventists, Mormons, and neocharismatics. The strength of these groups has been widely studied and greatly admired. But the direct application of sectarian standards to mainline churches creates two kinds of problems: First, it is doubtful if churches can become sects by their own volition. The social dynamic seems to move in the opposite direction, from sect to church. Second, neither churches nor sects have been notably effective in reaching a third type of religious expression (as defined by Ernst Troeltsch et al.*), namely the individualized mysticism of the New and Young Believers. If the mainline denominations wish to reach the populations that once supported their congregations, the Kelley thesis appears to be an inappropriate stance to take. Sectarian theology does not seem to be compatible with the Post-Materialist who expresses faith in a spiritual and mystic religion.

The Kelley thesis, beyond its particulars, commends the mainline churches to be specific in faith, sensitive to human need, open to social mobility, and decisive in social witness. As a sectarian theology, it does not explain the decline of mainline denominations, nor does it offer much promise as a means of making effective contact with the "lost members" of mainline churches.

*For a helpful discussion of this theme, see Colin Campbell, "The Secret Religion of the Educated Classes," *Sociological Analysis,* 1978, 39:2.

## Cultural Christian Churches

The church growth movement, as described by C. Peter Wagner (UCGD, chap. 12), has defined the primary task of the church-to-be membership growth—in both numbers and spiritual depth. However, most of the publication and discussion surrounding this movement has centered on numerical growth. The movement is research-oriented, with a unique emphasis upon identifying the sociological factors that correlate with receptivity to the gospel of Jesus Christ, defined by increasing church membership. If the principal task of the church is growth, then the tools of sociology and of anthropology are combined in the discipline of missiology to provide data for more effective membership growth. In the face of overwhelming data which suggests that social context will set the limits of church growth, the church is not powerless. Churches can choose the social context in which they will grow. For more effective communication of the gospel, churches should target their mission to the kind of people who can hear them best. Rather than arguing against the social contextual analysis of membership growth, the Church Growth Institute makes an ally of the facts.

By combining the motivations of church members with the realities of social context and with his own concern for healthy churches, Peter Wagner has articulated several principles of growth that have evolved from experience:

1. *Commitment.* The church must want to grow. The pastor particularly must be committed to this top priority, and the members must be mobilized. Growth must be the spiritual commitment for which the church is willing to work and work hard.

2. *Identify our people.* Based on the principle of the homogeneous unit, church members must look for others who are like themselves in values, culture, background, and religious expectations. "People blindness" is a sickness that

prevents persons in a church from recognizing the significant cultural differences that separate people into groups, differences which tend to obstruct the communication of the gospel message.

3. *Receptivity.* Within the people, those who are the most receptive should be identified and contacted first. It is equally important for the congregation to be prepared to receive additional members. The congregation must be a Big Enough church—Big Enough in the number of activities and in physical facilities. In attitude, the members must be ready to accept new people, and in organization, the church must be ready to provide different levels of experience.

4. *Priority.* Much as the first principle is an affirmation of willingness to grow, the final principle is a willingness to cut unproductive elements from church programs, such as too much cooperation with other churches. Target populations must be chosen for their potential productivity; those that are resistant should be bypassed to make more fruitful use of time. Several community situations are specifically mentioned as unproductive: people engaged in socioeconomic mobility (lift principle), changing urban communities (ethnikitis sickness), and disintegrating rural communities (old age).

The homogeneous unit, the distinguishing feature of the church growth movement, has wide statistical support from the current research of national denominations, particular congregations, and individual religious values. Growing congregations appear to depend upon finding a source of "our people," usually defined as a particular socioeconomic and cultural group. For mainline churches, growth correlates with affluent families that have school-age children, who live in separate homes. Community change—such as racial differences, economic decline, housing deterioration, or commercial intrusion—is associated with membership decline. The statistics on mainline churches strongly support the homogeneous unit principle. Even when a congregation appears to be diversified, a unifying core of ethnic background, middle-class values, or theological viewpoint can usually be seen as the anchor of homogeneity. The church growth movement did not invent the concept, but it did baptize it as acceptable to the Lord.

The phenomenal growth of many suburban congregations provides a textbook model for the church growth movement. The suburban context has already screened the population for socioeconomic homogeneity. Further, the congregations are large enough to provide many Big Enough churches, with facilities, staff, and programs to serve a wide variety of ages and interests, from small cells to large celebrations. These suburban congregations have not fallen into the evils of "hypercooperation" with other churches. They are very competitive. With this style they will grow as long as the community keeps expanding.

Conversely, the Church Growth Institute specifically warns the church about false expectations for growth in communities that are more diversified—"ethnikitis" in the changing city, "old age" in declining rural areas, and "lift" in areas of mobile, wealthy families. The middle-class suburban church remains the movement's prototype of church growth. In those communities the churches grow—all denominations—and continue to grow as long as "our kind of people" are available.

Three comments might be helpful to set the Church Growth Institute in perspective for mainline church programs: First, it works. Given all the proper conditions, especially the appropriate social context and the religious commitment of pastor and members, Wagner and others have been able to articulate many significant elements that are essential for growing congregations in the socialization of new suburban communities. Further, they have emphasized the importance of priorities for the congregations and for the denomination. They have properly criticized the failure of nerve that seized several mainline denominations in the mid and late 1960s, inhibiting

55

the development of new congregations where people needed religious witness. In faith, Church Growth leaders were aggressive and confident when many other religious leaders were self-critical and undecided; they have confronted the mainline denominations with a kind of religious pragmatism, saying in effect, "If there is a will (divine), there is a way (human)."

Second, the Church Growth Institute has misunderstood the nature of mainline theology. They have confused priorities with what Martin Marty has called Private Religion, which places a primary emphasis on traditional family values, work efficiency, and personal morality. Certainly mainline denominations have held these standards of faith to be central to the Christian life.

But mainline churches have never been content to restrict religious concerns to private religion. As James Smylie makes clear (UCGD, chap. 3), since their formative crisis in the era of the Reformation, these mainline denominations have proclaimed the Word of God to be an important measure of public as well as private morality, to be as definitive for monarchs and magistrates as for individual citizens. Mainline Christian churches—Catholic and Protestant—have never restricted God to the private lives of individuals. They have a heritage of public religion as well as private faith.

The Church Growth Institute, with its pragmatic insights and emphasis upon numerical church growth, has tempted many congregations to lay aside other tasks for the singular urgency of membership recruitment. Studies of mainline denominations offer no significant support for the necessity of highly organized membership committees. Growth often occurs without a concentrated effort per se. For the most part, growing churches are characterized by strong worship and diversified program, by an effective pastor and an enthusiastic congregation. That growing churches do more things and feel better about what they are doing is a generalization which must

be modified when we turn to specific types of church programming, in chapters 5 and 6.

Mainline churches witness to their faith by caring for their
communities. In metropolitan areas growing congregations
that are most "distinctive" are most apt to be involved in
community affairs. In suburban communities growing
churches are as significantly involved in social concerns as they
are in recruitment of new members. The theological orientation
of mainline churches includes a strong tradition of caring for
the community. Singular attention to membership growth
appears to be disruptive.

Third, the homogeneous unit does provide a description of
the mainline churches, but that description is a judgment upon
the church's failure to embrace as Christ's family "all people
who come in the name of the Lord." The body of Christ is not
predetermined by the exterior similarity of social class and
cultural background. The people of God are not simply the
fractured reflections of divisions that exist on earth. The very
effectiveness of the homogeneous principle is, according to
church theology, both catholic and reformed, a denial of the
fullness of Christ at any given time and place on earth.

Peter Wagner, among others, has introduced confusion
between his call for homogeneous congregational development and the worldly separation that is advocated by Dean
Kelley. More accurately, the positions of these two men are in
opposition. Wagner has suggested that the church growth
movement is, in the terms of H. Richard Niebuhr, a theology *of*
culture. But in his enthusiasm to spread the gospel through
homogeneous contacts, Wagner reduces the focus from Christ
in all culture to a Christ in "my" culture. Thus, Wagner ends
with a theological rationale for separate cells of Christians who
are "like me." He calls on Kelley for theological support.

Kelley, however, moves in the opposite direction. He begins
with a theological rationale for why Christians should be

separated from the world as it is and provides biblical criteria for Christian distinctiveness. In Niebuhr's terms, he offers a Christian alternative to culture: Christ *against* culture. He then invites all the world to join in the Christian Way. Wagner begins with sociological class and concludes with self-justifying separatism. Kelley begins with biblical separatism and proceeds with an invitation for all the world to join. Both Wagner and Kelley are concerned with the future of the Christian church, but there the similarity ends. They begin in opposite places, and move in opposite directions. The confusion of Kelley and Wagner has led to an uncritical acceptance of the principles of the Church Growth Institute. Neither Wagner nor Kelley represents the mediating position of the mainline Protestant churches.

### Exceptional Growth

In stark contrast with the declining membership of other mainline denominations of the National Council of Churches, the Southern Baptist Convention has been frequently cited as a model of exceptional growth that stood against the tide. Without detracting in any way from the Christian commitment of Baptist members and leaders through which the Spirit works, the growth of the Southern Baptist Convention seems more like a fortuitous combination of all the major factors involved in church growth focused in a single denomination.

The Southern Baptists are concentrated in southern areas of the country, where church attendance is traditionally higher and the total population is expanding. Further, they tend to have larger families, maintain a lower socioeconomic status, and remain in the communities of their birth. As a denomination, the Baptists have a heritage of private religion based on separatist, sectarian theology, born out of bitter experience in Europe and in America. Their faith has contributed to the stability of community mores and to the continuity of human relationships. Kelley's characteristics of strength are part of their religious tradition. Wagner's identity of a homogeneous unit reflects their way of life. They provide a providential combination of congregations that is theologically strong and culturally settled.

Moreover, in a time of declining trust in national institutions, the Southern Baptist Convention retained the initiative for starting new churches through existing congregations. Phillip Jones (UCGD, chap. 7) notes that a new congregation is developed by an existing "mother church." Lacking national organization, staff, and resources to begin new churches, the responsibility rests with the local association and congregation. The newborn mission remains joined to the mother congregation until the younger church has the strength to live alone. Although this process creates problems in statistical reporting, it gives local churches the fundamental satisfaction of the labor new birth requires. Part of the weakness of other denominations may lie in a bureaucracy that has deprived local congregations of opportunities to flex the muscles of their faith in public. As denominational policy, in the decade following 1965, the Southern Baptist Convention did not show the same decline in the number of new churches started when other mainline churches were distracted from new church development. The initiative remained with the local congregations and area associations.

In short, the Southern Baptists were in the right places, and they were organized and motivated to make the most of their opportunities. They grew when other mainline churches declined, and they continue to grow in every part of the country.

Unfortunately for the purity of theological sectarianism, success breeds corruption. Dean Kelley quotes from John Wesley: "I do not see how it is possible in the nature of things for any true religion to continue long."

One might almost project such a future for conservative churches in general and for the Southern Baptist Convention in

59

particular. The numerical growth and financial success of membership might corrode the disciplines of the church and might encourage deterioration of the wall that divides private religion from public responsibility. The election of Jimmy Carter and the rise of the neoevangelicals have, in different ways, already indicated denominational movement in this direction. In time this giant denomination, even with its deep sectarian roots and its aversion to denominational hierarchy, could be swamped by the responsible middle class and neutralized by prosperity and pluralism. As success nudges the Baptists toward the middle of the religious spectrum, the older denominations must move over and make room for another style of mediating the eternal grace of God. Such a scenario is possible, and I believe it is in process. When it happens, and for those congregations where it has already occurred, membership statistics will look more like those of other mainline churches.

## *Mediating Christian Values*

Traditionally, mainline Protestant churches have not believed that God could be pushed to the sidelines—either in a personal life-style or in the broad arena of public policy. It is therefore no accident that the declining churches were those denominations which had supported the old Federal Council of Churches. These ecumenical organizations proposed to affirm the sovereignty of God in the public arena, as well as in the private affairs of individuals. As James Smylie has pointed out (UCGD, chap. 3), most of these denominations that are now declining once enjoyed an establishment position in the nations in which they emerged at the time of the Reformation. They felt responsible for the total life of the culture. By contrast, sectarian faith groups were not establishment; they were often persecuted, and they developed a primary concern for the interior religious life of the individual Christian. The once-establishment churches became denominations, yielding their monopolies of prestige and power but not their concern for public affairs. This pluralistic Protestant establishment ultimately evolved into the celebrated Judeo-Christian affirmations of religious liberty and the separation (but not isolation) of church and state.

Historically, mainline churches have been mediators of religious values. Sometimes they have struggled to unite a troubled nation, as in World War II, in the face of fascism, and to a lesser extent in the Korean conflict, in the face of the Communist threat. Sometimes these mediating churches have seen their prophetic role as challenging the abuse of power, as in the institutional racism of the civil rights conflict or in the militarism of the Vietnam War. In all these conditions the mainline churches perceived their function to be the same: that of mediating religious values which provide the basis for Christian life in a secular world. Whether the actions of the church are preaching from the pulpit or counseling for marriage, offering the sacraments or praying beside a hospital bed, teaching in church school or organizing a scout troop, mainline denominations have considered themselves mediators of basic Christian values and insights, which are as important in the private lives of individuals as they are in the public policies of the nation.

Church size, membership growth or decline, or the appeal to influential members have never been considered criteria by which mainline churches measured their effectiveness, as Robert A. Evans observed (UCGD, chap. 13). Nor have they measured their health by the theological consistency of statements or the absolute conformity of their constituent parts. Mainline denominations have lived in the middle, between historic revelation and the continual unfolding of new, unanticipated human conditions for which the Word of God must be made relevant. Every day the scripture is fresh because the world to which it speaks is different. Every Sunday the Word must be preached, because the people of God must mediate the Spirit in the midst of human need.

In the Reformed tradition, God cannot be driven to the sidelines. The church is the mediator in the middle, where we are saved by the grace of God alone. Dean Kelley is tempting because he is a theological sectarian who seeks a community who knows its faith is pure, because it is biblical. Peter Wagner is popular because he is a sociological sectarian who seeks a community who knows its kind is pure, because they are "like us." But mainline churches are not sectarians. They affirm the ambiguities of mediating the fresh grace of God in a constantly changing human world. The Reformed tradition of the mediating church in the middle suggests heavy responsibilities but prohibits ultimate answers. Faithfulness is not a dogma, but a way of living. It appeals to some people, but not to everyone.

### Low Middle Ground

Just as the Southern Baptist Convention provided a model for strong cultural churches, as proposed by Kelley and Wagner, so the church membership trends from the western United States appear to support what Hoge and Marty have called the collapse of the middle. Whereas church attendance in the southern region has consistently been above 70 percent of the population for the past fifty years, church participation in the West has been below 40 percent over the same period of time. Studies of the congregations in mainline denominations do not show that growing churches in the western region are more or less conservative than in any other part of the country. In the West a smaller percentage of the population belongs to mainline denominations than in any other region. Moreover, close examination of the data suggests that western congregations are more likely to state their positions on theological and social issues. They appear to have a more clearly defined theological identity.

In general, the culture of the West, from California to Alaska, seems more supportive of disciplined congregations that are actively evangelical and theologically conservative. This area supports few mainline churches, and these are more radicalized into social and theological positions. The culture in the West includes a large proportion of New and Young Believers who affirm their individualism and who are not attracted to religious institutions. Under these conditions, the function of mainline churches to mediate religious values is greatly reduced. In a highly polarized society, the mediating position is very lonely.

### The Choice of a Future

What is the future for mainline churches? We might follow the early Baptist model and become strong cultural enclaves of religion. We might learn from the New Young Believers and individualize the faith until we have no need for religious institutions. For some people, each of these choices makes sense. There is a third scenario in which mainline churches can learn to be more effective where they are, as mediators in the middle. This requires a shift in attitude on the part of many mainline leaders and not a few church members. We can treat the boom of the 1950s as if it were a great party that is past and recover from the hangover of too many members too quickly departed. We can begin by affirming our historic position as mediators of grace in the ambiguous middle of social need and human crisis. In the middle we have two strong constituencies for which we can accept pastoral responsibility:

First, our members are with us in our mediation posture. These are the mainline Christians who call themselves con- servative but who continue to organize for the poor and the dispossessed. The United Church of Christ noted that congregations which are theologically diverse and socially active provide members with the highest correlation of personal satisfaction. Apparently, in these congregations love is not enough, for the loving person is also engaged in articulating a personal faith and in advocating for a just society. All our studies indicate that the higher the income and education of the membership, the more likely the church is involved in both conservative theology and social concerns. The faithfulness of mainline churches has been maintained by the members as much as it has by pastors. Our people are pluralistic. They hope that the church is bigger than their personal lives and private values.

Second, the church in the middle has the greatest opportunity to minister to the needs of that body of people who have not bothered to belong to the church but who have retained a positive faith in the power of God. In the middle we have a large constituency who believe but no longer belong. These people have been characterized by their strong personal values and diversified experimental life-styles. They seek the help of the church only temporarily, only in the times of "passage." They need a kind of intimacy that does not make long-term demands. Often they seek only the counsel of the anonymous stranger. These are the religious silent minority who know that they might need the church—but never know when. They believe in the importance of the church, but not in the necessity for belonging. The survival of particular congregations depends upon our ability to persuade this silent neighborhood constituency to lend their support, even though they are not members.

Local congregations may change, but they will not disappear—in some aspects they may emerge stronger and more self-reliant from the transition. The local congregation may become more like the Jewish synagogue, with its faithful few to carry on the routine activities and its overflow crowds at the festivals and sacred days. Historically, the Protestant church provided such a spiritual leaven. When America was born, most of its founders were not members of "mainline churches"; they were deists—much like the "invisible religion" of our own time. Churches were not irrelevant, and clergy were among the movers of the nation. But no one expected all the religious people to be in church or the churches to be interested only in religion.

How can the church survive with a membership inside and a constituency outside? To these programmatic implications we must turn our attention.

# CHAPTER 5

# *Programming to Include the Outsider*

If social context sets general limits of growth for any given congregation, then someone forgot to tell the churches that are reaching their maximum, even exceeding their limits. When new members are asked why they joined a particular congregation, their responses are often vague and embarrassingly fuzzy: "There is something special about this place." "It's warm." "It's alive." "It's spiritual." "It's familiar." "It's exciting."

Growing congregations have a spirit that is distinguishable from dying churches. Some churches which are declining in membership have that same spark, even in the face of overwhelming difficulties. Other congregations, even in areas of maximum growth potential, are barely limping along. There is a spiritual quality in some congregations that will make the difference, if the social context allows any room for growth at all.

Programming in the local congregation is a combination of three elements: the spiritual quality of the members and leaders, the theological orientation of the congregation and denomination, and the community social context for which the ministry is intended. This chapter explores a few program implications for mainline churches that seek to serve their own membership within the church and that wish to reach out to a larger constituency of those who are sympathetic with the church, but who are not members. Implications for six areas of local church programming and for denominational support in developing these congregational programs are touched on. In each case the minimal research available is noted, and you are encouraged to use your imagination to apply it to congregations you know and love.

## *Worship*

Worship is the crossroads of congregational feelings. Although it is the focal point for both growing and declining congregations, there is a difference. Growing congregations have positive feelings about worship, while worship is a source of controversy in declining churches (UCGD, chaps. 9 and 10). Of all the elements of church programming, in all sorts of churches, feelings about worship are consistently among the most significant factors associated with growth or decline. Either something special happens in worship or it doesn't.

*Identity in worship.* For many church members, Sunday morning worship is significant in the rhythm and pace of the whole week. To test its importance, simply suggest that the time of the service be moved to a "more convenient hour." The style of worship reaffirms the Christian identity of church members, whether that style is liturgical music, or center-pulpit preaching, classical Puritan prayers, or intimate sharing by members of the congregation. The style of worship is "the way we do it around here."

Worship is like a mirror to the members of a congregation: they know who they are by how they feel about worship. Worship cannot make a congregation healthy, but it can tell the people when they are ill. There is a world of difference between traditional ritual and empty routine, between being proper and being dull. High liturgy can be dramatic, not simply stuffy. Liturgical warmth does not need to be sloppy or thoughtless. Freshness and excitement in worship depends more on the presence of the Spirit than on calculated creativity. Effort and resources invested in worship are well spent. Quality makes a difference.

*Diversity in worship.* Mainline churches are faced with special problems because of diversity in the congregation. No single appeal has brought members into the congregation, except the lordship of Christ for all the world. Warren Hartman, in a study of congregations of the United Methodist Church (UCGD, chap. 2), has identified various "audiences" that participate in a typical Sunday morning worship, each with slightly different expectations. He lists these audiences as follows: persons moved primarily by fellowship (17%), by evangelistic concerns (11%), by study (8%), by social concerns (6%), and the others (58%), who combined two or more interests. Different programs in the life of any congregation speak more directly to these varied interests, but worship is central to them all. In some ways it must honor and embrace the diversity of interests, without endorsing everything in which each group might become involved. Mainline churches are all these things and more.

"I want no apologies about my faith," a young woman said to a pastor who was trying to excuse the diversity of viewpoints in a particular congregation. "I want to belong to a faith that is bigger than I am. That's why I joined this church." Mainline churches embrace a diversity of faith within the congregation and display that diversity in the Sunday worship. That we do not all agree on everything is basic to mainline theological appeal. In worship we admit our differences and celebrate our oneness in Christ—who is big enough to embrace us all.

*The Word in the world.* Mainline churches seek to mediate Christian values that are helpful to individuals and are important for public policy. For them, public worship is a particularly significant event. Since everything is grist for theological reflection, pastors and worship leaders are often uncertain about what is appropriate to include in which services of worship. If the Word is to be relevant, it must include the world in the worship experience. Worship is not withdrawal from the world, but an affirmation of God in the midst. This approach produces uncomfortable prayers and disquieting sermons and not a few sleepless nights for the clergy. Pastors and members should find some comfort in the clear evidence that worship is still worth fighting about. Growing churches generate an excitement about worship that gives focus to the rest of their lives.

*Different times and places.* For many people the most significant and memorable worship experiences are not on Sunday mornings, but at seasonal events and in the passages of their lives. Once-a-week Christians need to appreciate that theirs is not the only way to faithfully respond to the lordship of Christ.

Ancient Christian cultures and religious communities provide examples of seasonal rhythm in worship. These include the Christmas celebration, which brings the family together for the beginning of the fresh year as Christians; the Easter celebration of God's conquest of death in Jesus Christ; Pentecost; Thanksgiving; and special festivals that are significant in the lives of particular congregations. For these celebrations a much larger community gathers to share the love of God than is possible on any given Sunday.

The religious traditions from which we come suggest that such celebrations should not be confined to any particular place, but that they gain in significance when they are observed in different settings and are in touch with the things of the community. Ancient blessings and judgments, greetings and sorrows, were movable feasts, incorporating more of the people and the living space than just the walls of the "sanctuary."

The Church Growth Institute in its analysis of congregational readiness for growth, has emphasized the need for
celebrations to bring larger groups of Christians together to
share the excitement of significant, worshipful events. Such
celebrations have played an important part in the history of
mainline churches, but in this era of self-doubt these festivals
have been conspicuous by their absence. At the same time, the
more evangelical denominations have magnified their cer-
emonies through the use of television. Celebrations not only
bring self-confidence to the faith-filled members, but they also
provide a warm bonfire for the anonymous religious seeker to
come a little closer.

*Individual covenants.* If mainline churches are to reach the
mobile society and the mystical believer, several levels of
membership may need to be offered. In response to new
life-styles, sensitive congregations have developed a variety of
contracts to which prospective members may make commitment as moved by the Spirit, but also limited by other commitments in their lives. Such contracts are part of our Puritan
heritage on the one side and of revival religion on the other.
Worship is the natural context. In one congregation the
"extended family of faith" includes kindred spirits who share
"in the Spirit and the ministry of the congregation." In another,
the members are invited to sign the compact annually, in
worship, on Pentecost Sunday. One member allows that "it
makes the pastor a little nervous each spring, but it all works out
OK."

Not everyone is touched by the worship experience, and
many find it difficult to relate to the congregation through such
corporate activities. For those who believe without belonging,
worship may be the last step in their journey to membership—not the first. Members of the church constituency (nonmembers) who have come to the pastor for counseling may find that their relationship in the context of Sunday
morning worship is too distant. People who have undergone the

emotional high of a spiritual retreat or the rediscovery of affection in a marriage renewal weekend may find the formality of public worship offensive to their sense of Christian intimacy. Some are beyond participation in public worship and others are not yet ready for it.

For most who attend, however, and for the life of the congregation as a whole, worship remains the formative experience at the center of feelings and commitment.

## *The Church School*

The importance attached to the church school is second only to public worship. Teaching Christian values to children is considered by many to be the most significant activity in the life of the church. As noted earlier, in chapter 2, the trend of church school participation in one year will be repeated in denominational membership five years later.

*Continuity of the Faith.* Children in the church school are symbolic of a fundamental value that lies at the heart of mainline Protestant churches. Church emphasis upon the church school is the key to appreciating the conservative quality of American religious commitments. Mainline churches are carriers of the most intimate values and experience: the sanctity of life and the importance of the family, rites of passage and divine support in times of crisis, the meaning of labor and the permanence of love. Children in the church school are the recipients of these precious values, learned more by experience than discussion. For the congregation, the children are the promise of the future yet to be, the assurance that what has been important to the members will be carried on by the next generation. It is not surprising that all indexes of family values correlate with church strength and growth. Conversely, the issues that most quickly arouse the church are those which deal with marriage, divorce, and alternative life-styles; with alcohol, drugs, and mind-expanding experiences; with homosexuality, abortion, and the ERA—all rationally far apart, but emotionally loaded with threats to what church members have experienced as basic Christian family virtues.

Thus, the church school is a source of pride and promise for the future for older members of the congregation. For teachers and parents, however, it is often the crucible in which the elements of both the past and present values are crushed and mixed emotionally, with unpredictable consequences.

*Church school for nonmembers.* The relationship between declining birthrate and church school/church membership has been carefully studied and argued by Dean Hoge and David Roozen (UCGD, chaps. 4 and 5). In essence, they suggest that churches do not grow or decline because of changes in the population, but rather the birthrate changes because of changing values. These changes in attitudes toward families and children have been noted in the discussion of Young Believers (see chapter 3). Hoge does not speculate about the causes of these value shifts, when they might change again, or what direction they may take.

For the present, congregations are faced with a substantial decrease in the number of children available for the traditional educational efforts of the church school, with its implied depressed self-image for the life of the whole congregation. In response, many congregations have rediscovered the church school as it was at the time of its inception, more than a century ago—an instrument of membership outreach through children. Bus ministries have developed in staid old congregations, and even children in middle- and upper-middle-class communities are being picked up. Evidently, parents who feel no personal need for religious participation have willingly permitted their children to be collected for a Sunday experience. These programs have met with such parental support that they appear to mean as much to the parents who do not attend as to the children who do.

72

In the 1950s parents brought their children. Now, in many cases, children bring their parents, if they come at all.

*Church schools for adults.*   Fortunately, from one perspective, not all growing congregations have growing church schools. Effective congregations in the cities and in the older suburbs have found ways to maintain strong church programs and to expand their membership without reliance on the family image of the church school. Churches in older suburban areas show a consistent choice of programs that offer adults a more challenging Christian faith. Like the city churches, congregations in these stable suburban communities gather membership from adults of all ages, from childless couples and single parents, from the whole range of people who have personal needs without available resources.

Family values are still held in supreme reverence in mainline churches, but Roozen has noted a shift in the family cycle of church participation. At one time older couples decreased their church participation when the children left the nest; now older adults are more likely to participate than families with children still at home. Many churches have adjusted their church school to meet these changing life-styles, where wives are more apt to be working, where divorce has broken and mixed the family pattern, where employment has kept families constantly on the move, where single adults sometimes live together. Occasionally, singles even adopt children and look for a church school to help rear them.

For more than a century the church school has been the bedrock mediator of faith within the mainline churches, especially those that lacked weekday parochial schools. Mainline churches, especially in older communities, must be Big Enough institutionally to absorb the diversity and Big Enough spiritually to absorb the changes. Some congregations with few available children have moved into patterns of "family education." Others have helped to develop extended-

73

family kinds of kinship between teenagers and elderly members. Many churches have abandoned the church school as such, since they were haunted by the memories of better times. Some have found even more significant ways of sharing in the development of small groups within the congregation.

## *Small-group Experiences*

Small groups are third in importance in growing congregations (UCGD, chaps. 9 and 10) but fall far below the expectations that many have invested in this style of sharing feelings and actions. The Church Growth Institute in particular has vigorously advocated the use of small groups as a means of building church membership for programmatic reasons—it works. However, small groups are most effective in proportion to population mobility and density; the more frequently people move or the greater the number of people to be assimilated, the more helpful small groups have proven in growing churches. They are widely used in growing suburbs, often used in crowded cities, rarely used (or at least not identified) in smaller cities and in town and country churches.

*Identity through small groups.* In larger congregations, people may officially join the church, but emotionally they belong to a small group. It is not uncommon to find prayer groups and Bible study cells among the most frequent expressions of group life in growing congregations. These groups are important for mutual support of the members and for trusted communication concerning the goals and programs of the larger congregational activities. Some groups must be open to ensure assimilation of new members. Assimilation groups are especially effective if they provide common tasks, such as meal preparation or church work days. Other groups must be closed to new members, in order to permit a deeper level of sharing in the fears and faith of mature Christian living.

*Accommodation of diversity.* As the Church Growth Insti-

74

tute has clearly stated, growing congregations must be Big Enough to affirm and absorb many interests that are important to some members, but appear to be irrelevant or inappropriate to others. Small groups are the organizational way that churches affirm their own diverse elements without endorsing each of their separate interests. Small groups permit congregations to "count only 'yes' votes," as Lyle E. Schaller says; if there is enough interest for a group, let it happen.

Beyond the immediate membership of the congregation, small groups provide the church with a means to support community activities without sponsoring additional programs. In this way the church may provide support groups for single parents or meditation experiences with yoga disciplines or access to legal aid counseling. For mainline churches, small groups have provided the umbrella for many caring programs that the congregation could not sponsor.

Growing mainline churches have a significantly larger number of community activities using the church facilities on a regular basis.

*Temporary covenants.* In communities where the population mobility makes long-term commitments difficult, the number and variety of small groups with specific purposes and limited life spans make immediate assimilation easier for the recent arrival. In stable populations the congregation is often exceeded in size by the church constituency, which is made up of people who have lived in the community so long that they feel they belong by virtue of knowing so many members (and pastors) and by sharing many experiences in the building—a kind of ecclesiastical squatters' rights. In more mobile populations the churches are frequently much smaller than the total shown on the membership rolls. Often the names of members who have moved are not taken off the membership rolls, and recently arrived neighbors do not yet feel they are a part of the congregation.

In highly mobile communities, intense group experiences,

such as weekend retreats or special summer trips, can develop the trust and mutual understanding that could mature slowly in more settled cultures. Both members and nonmembers can share these experiences and grow in faith together.

*Cost and income.* Does this additional community activity distract from the primary purpose and dissipate the resources of the congregation? Both the Presbyterian and the United Church of Christ studies (UCGD, chaps. 9 and 10) attempted to determine the relative effectiveness of congregations that had clarity of focus, as opposed to congregations with broad interests and a wide range of activities. They discovered separately that most growing congregations were involved in more activities, not fewer, and offered more choices. Interest in one activity kindled enthusiasm for another.

Financially, many community activities contribute to the church and do so willingly. In fact, groups that make financial donations may feel more a part of the church than those to whom space is provided free. At the same time, some members of the congregation will take special pride in the knowledge that the congregation is supporting these "additional ministries."

*New members.* Not the least important in the development of small groups for members and constituents is the prospect that nonmembers will find themselves so much at home in the life of the church group that they may wish to join the congregation. In some cases members have joined a congregation on the last Sunday before they are transferred, because joining was seen as a symbolic act for something that had already happened months or even years earlier. For mainline churches that are seeking to make contact with the New Believers, the clarity of membership is secondary to the common base of shared experiences.

### Dropouts

Although dropouts have not been a major source of loss for mainline churches, they have received considerable attention in the search for clues to the meaning of membership. The results are not clear-cut, but there appears to be a general consensus from a variety of perspectives (UCGD, chap. 2).

*An emotional commitment.* Similar to the responses of new members when asked why they joined the church, the memories of dropouts are fuzzy and inarticulate. Often those who are the most introspective offer the vaguest responses, supported by descriptions of feelings involved, which seem to be more emotional than theological. Pastors and church officers who stand by and observe class after class of new members may have underestimated the emotional lift many people feel on entry to a church. With joining comes an openness to friendship and a vulnerability to disappointment.

*Relationships.* Dropouts who remain in the vicinity of the church frequently cite broken relationships as their main reason for leaving. Some former Presbyterians list their reasons in this order: (1) loss of important friendships, (2) disappointment with pastoral relationship, (3) theological disagreement with the church, and (4) a need for personal religious independence. As a result of interviewing a sampling of former Methodists, John S. Savage was able to establish early incidents in which dropouts felt alienated from a significant relationship—usually with the pastor, family member, or another member of the church. If personal alienation is allowed to fester, the entire church relationship will be infected. Unresolved personal tensions play a major role in causing people to drop out of a church.

Donald Metz has noted that a high incidence of dropping out can be traced to strained or broken relationships that lie beyond the membership of the congregation. Other family members were usually identified as the source of conflict.

People join congregations, at least in part, for social satisfactions. They leave when these social expectations are damaged or are left unfulfilled. Growing congregations have found ways—formal and informal—by which the social needs of individuals can be recognized, their achievement needs can be honored, and their social status can remain intact. Without these three strokes—recognition, esteem, and a sense of belonging—members will become frustrated and will withdraw.

*Theological reasons.* Although theological conflicts as reasons for dropping out of church are not offered as frequently or with as much emotion as the feelings listed above, they are still important. Some dropouts mention a theological conflict with the social involvement of the congregation; for them, religion is a more private affair. Others note the absence of contemporary worship or the financial preoccupation of church leadership as explanations for their withdrawal. Generally, membership dropouts were far more apt to leave in boredom than in disagreement. The challenges of the church, if any, had not made contact with priorities among the member's own goals and values.

Implicit in membership withdrawal is a curious double standard. When people unite with a congregation, they resist suggesting personal need or social satisfactions as causes for joining. They consciously relate church membership with program participation and religious values. When they leave, however, they are more likely to blame a breakdown in personal relationships.

## *Organizing for New Members*

New members are important—to the Lord, to themselves, and for the boost they give the ministry of the congregation. Some churches are not ready or even willing to seek new members or to include them if they should come (UCGD, chap. 16).

*New-member committees.* As already noted, churches with new-member committees do not grow any faster than churches without such groups. Even though there is some evidence that these committees may be counterproductive, their presence reflects a need. However, they are not a substitute for the membership-wide responsibility to invite others.

Frequently, such committees represent a recognition that the character of the community has changed. Their efforts to contact prospective members must become more focused and intentional. New-member committees may appear to be counterproductive because they are often found in congregations where the social context makes church growth almost impossible, or in congregations where the larger membership has lost its enthusiasm about the ministry it shares. Many times such groups are symptomatic of deeper difficulties that the congregation must face head on.

*New-member sources.*   New members will probably come from the same sources that have served the church in the past and through personal contact. Although mainline denominations might struggle with the social and the cultural limitations of the homogeneous unit, most congregations are composed of people who share the same world view, the same personal values, and the same family-friendship networks. New sources can be opened through conscious penetration into other areas of neighborhood, business, and school. For example, day-care services or meal programs for the elderly can tap a new supply of members for some congregations.

The church school continues to be a point of contact with many new families. Parents of school-age children are still receptive to permitting the church to teach their children basic Christian values. But both demographic and value changes suggest that the church school will not provide the channel to membership which it has in the past generation.

Adults of all ages provide the most challenging new source for church membership. In the past the family cycle provided one basic entry: parents of school-age children. The disruption of that traditional pattern has made all adults almost equally responsive to congregations who speak their language.

*Value conflict and assimilation.*   The church that targets its

79

population has a better chance of attracting new members. This requires the congregation to develop a relatively clear concept of their present membership; a close look generally entails hard work and generates surprises. Further, the selection of a population target requires a hard look at the community—which is usually more promising than it seems from a distance. Realism is the basis for growth.

Growing congregations maximize their own resources in relation to community potential, but they do not feel that their membership reflects a mirror image of the community. Growth most frequently occurs where church members share a concern for similar issues with prospective members, but do not necessarily provide the same answers. The church must speak the language of its community without abdicating basic Christian values. Members and constituents share a concern, but not necessarily an answer.

For example, the nuclear family may be American, but it is not the only biblical pattern for family groups. With the New and Young Believers, the church needs to share in the common search for new life-styles that witness to the love of God through similar and different patterns.

For example, in the past church membership may have been a lifetime commitment for people who remained in one community all their lives. In this mobile society, commitment to God may be forever, but membership in a congregation will change several times for the typical mainline church family. We need words to describe these new realities.

### Local Church Leadership

When a typical church member moves almost as frequently as the average church pastor (between five and eight years), the stability of a local congregation is provided officially by the leadership board and unofficially by the choir, the women's association, and the adult Bible class.

*Official leadership.* In a situation of such fluidity, members of the official boards must often carry the burden of institutional functions—church school organization, group meetings, building maintenance, financial management, and the like. In congregations that embrace a diversity of interests and activities, the official board is often the focus of conflicting views and personalities. More so than program functions, a board's most important task is the legitimation of congregational diversity. This can be done through mutual understanding, clarity of purposes, commonly accepted goals, and public display of the pluralistic character of the congregation. In many ways a board must accept responsibility to authorize the diversity of mainline church activities.

*Unofficial leadership.* Apart from the visible government of the local church stands the network of the time-honored relationships. These old members have carried the congregation in hard times, and they have enjoyed the seasons of the heart. They may have the most difficulty adjusting to the stress of change—new members and new ways. Without their acceptance, pronouncements of the official board may be limited, but with their support "anything is possible."

In the midst of mainline church diversity, no one kind of issue can be identified as particularly dangerous: church members can disagree about worship, preaching, music, youth activities, social action, evangelistic styles, fund-raising techniques, and so on. The subject of disagreement is not a problem; it's the way in which they disagree that makes the difference.

## Denominational Policies

Denominational decisions have a direct impact on the growth and decline of individual congregations. Considerable space in UCGD has been devoted to the analysis of denominational strategies (especially chaps. 7 through 11) and to the theological rationale that guided these decisions (chaps. 3 and 12 through 16). No part of this discussion can be separated from denominational programs, since that is where ideas are translated into action. On balance, how have denominational policies affected church growth and decline?

*Affirmation of the American Way.* Old establishment churches brought with them to America their concern for the whole social order. With their emphasis on the Christian-American Way, they helped to build a patriotic pride in the success of individuals and in the progress of the nation. This affirmation of the American Life-style contributed to the growth of mainline churches through the 1950s and to their membership decline after 1965. It is doubtful if mainline churches could now break with their heritage, even if church councils took "definitive action."

*All things to all people.* Mainline churches reaffirmed their mediating position by attempting to embrace a wide variety of theological perspectives, racial/cultural hopes, political strategies, and programs for Christian witness. Only churches that conceived themselves as being "in the middle" could have taken the risk to mediate so many different values at once—in the name of Christian concern. Little wonder that the mainline churches lost their sense of direction and proudly tried to muddle through.

*New church starts.* The most serious casualty of the 1965-75 decade was the lost resolve among mainline churches to keep up the pace of organizing new congregations, even though growing suburban communities and a growing middle class among racial/ethnic groups in urban centers offered opportunities for mainline church membership growth. This lost initiative cost the mainline churches a decade of members and prospective young leaders, who were served by other denominations that were not willing to be distracted by the civic unrest of the times.

*Social issues.* By their statements on social issues and occasional involvement in social causes, mainline churches maintained their historic position as mediators of Christian values for the welfare of the whole society. This involvement caused considerable discussion but apparently did not bring about any significant numerical loss. Most members of the mainline churches agreed with the church's concern for the welfare of the whole society, although they may have disagreed with certain positions taken by the institutional church on particular issues.

*"Lost" members.* The decline in mainline church membership rolls resulted from a major shift of cultural values. Too few churches and too many issues may have made minor contributions to the decline, but the primary reason for membership losses is the emergence in the population of New and Young Believers who feel no particular need to join mainline churches, although they are the population from which mainline churches have drawn members in the past.

*Meaning of membership.* An ancient definition of church membership remains a major stumbling block for congregations that are trying to reach the New and Young Believers. Mainline denominations still offer a church membership that was developed for a localized population in a fixed, agrarian society. Cosmopolitan Christians, who live in a dynamic and technological society, need new ways of relating to the church without necessarily doing away with past procedures. Kindred spirits and an annual signing of the scroll seem appropriate options.

*Compelling visions.* The most costly action of mainline churches was not in doing too little or too much or the wrong thing. Rather, in the confusion, the churches seemed to forget why they were doing anything. Somehow, in all this activity, they lost the vision of Jesus Christ as Lord of the whole world. They lost the integrating faith that held the pieces in place. The church in the middle that loses the vision of the whole will appear divided and broken.

"It's not the dogma I want to pass on," a teacher of teenagers told me. "It's the challenge of Christ in the world. We owe these kids a challenge we can share with them, because it is bigger than all of us."

# CHAPTER 6

# *Something That Works*

"Give me something that works where I am," pleaded a pastor. After describing his situation in about two sentences, he said he needed more members and wanted a specific recommendation for a program that would be right for him and for his people. There was an awkward silence. "Well . . . "

Behind the pastor's genuine request lies two assumptions: First, that he could describe the situation with the kind of adjectives which would give an accurate assessment for program development. Second, that other churches with similar conditions could provide examples his congregation might be able to follow. The first is the problem of developing types of churches that have significant similar characteristics. The second is the discovery of the kinds of programs that fit the needs of those church types. These are considered in turn.

After working with church typologies and program patterns for several years, I have discovered one almost universal principle: It is relatively easy to type churches that other people attend and almost impossible to find a category that accurately fits the church in which we ourselves participate. Most people can describe alternative churches, with half a dozen different options, to their congregations. But when it comes to describing the church to which they belong, the list of telling terms is long, sometimes contradictory, and always incomplete.

Even if we could develop a typology of churches that satisfied most people, there is a spiritual dimension in discovering the "right program" for particular situations. Divine inspiration and human will have defied the computers and the program analysts. There is an art to choosing resources and the developing local church program. There is, finally, something intuitive, something spiritual, in the decisions to act and in the results that follow.

We can report how other people perceive church types as related to the communities in which the congregation is located. Further, we can report which programs have been effective for others in these settings. These are not sure-cure prescriptions for "something that works," but the experience of others may help a congregation to see themselves more clearly in their social situation and to imagine a more appropriate pattern of church programs.

### *Congregations in Community Context*

Social or community context is the basis for a typology of churches developed by Douglas Walrath (UCGD, chap. 11). Church membership, for most people, is intimately related to the broader pattern of relationships within their community. Patterns of participation in church life vary in different community settings: a downtown church has a different style of church program life than a church in a growing suburb or an old chapel in the country. Walrath identifies twelve metropolitan and nonmetropolitan church and community "types." Styles of pastoral care, congregational program, opportunities for membership growth, and the character of the church's ministry within one kind of community might prove awkward, embarrassing, or disastrous in another.

Having established the community context as the basis for

developing church types, Walrath proceeds to note differences in the ways congregations respond to their social contexts. Some churches dominate their communities and carry the life of that people embedded in their consciousness. Other congregations are passive toward their environment and let others make decisions for them. Still other congregations—such as a language or ethnic church, or a radically conservative congregation—withdraw from their community context. They attract a special kind of person from the community. Although they may find their identity in opposition to their social context, that context is still a point of reference.

The style of leadership adds a third dimension to the context and posture of a congregation. This provides a typology based on location, attitude, and leadership of the congregation. Thus, Walrath offers a panorama of congregations in context—mission, storefront, new church development, chapel, neighborhood church, and midtown cathedral all have context, character, and leadership. Although the number of church types that are embraced within this typology is exhausting (180 plus), the mix of factors provides a great many insights and far greater comfort when we find our niche.

Church members and pastors usually enjoy recalling experiences and identifying the differences in congregations that are located in several of these social settings. We have already noted the generally negative influence of radical population change upon congregations located in particular communities (chapter 2). Walrath expects that these social contextual influences will set the limits within which most congregations will develop program and attract membership: "Generally speaking, what leadership and program cannot do is enable a congregation to 'escape' from its group entirely, that is, to perform through time in a manner consistently different from the basic pattern for congregations of its type."

Some will find Walrath overly deterministic. We all know of

### FIGURE 7
### SOCIAL CONTEXT TYPOLOGY: GEOGRAPHICAL PATTERN

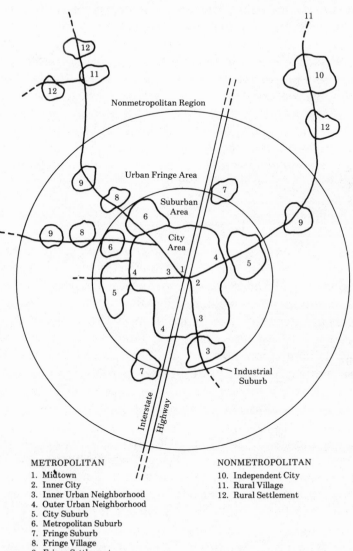

METROPOLITAN
1. Midtown
2. Inner City
3. Inner Urban Neighborhood
4. Outer Urban Neighborhood
5. City Suburb
6. Metropolitan Suburb
7. Fringe Suburb
8. Fringe Village
9. Fringe Settlement

NONMETROPOLITAN
10. Independent City
11. Rural Village
12. Rural Settlement

87

churches that have failed to fit expected patterns: churches that have thrived in inner city environments in the face of population declines and churches that have gone out of existence in suburban communities bulging at the seams with new residents looking for a church home. At the same time, Walrath points us to an important truth: What works in one setting can be a washout in another. Careful attention to the ecological or community context of the congregation can liberate concerned pastors and members from inappropriate guilt in some situations and from inordinate pride in others. By looking at churches that share somewhat similar community settings, we may be able to identify some of the keys to effective ministry appropriate to those diverse locations.

## Patterns of Growth

Especially successful churches have attracted innumerable case studies, but the learnings of one setting are not easily transferable to other congregations. Several denominations or regional groups have prepared studies that focus on a particular kind of congregation (small church, special ministry) or on a particular location (inner city, new suburbs). The results of larger denominational studies on a national or multiregional scale have been included in UCGD (chaps. 6 through 10). From two of these studies we can develop profiles of local congregational patterns that correlate with growth (chaps. 9 and 10).

Beginning in 1973 the United Church of Christ gathered extensive data on 263 congregations in Massachusetts and in Pennsylvania. These congregations were evaluated on six indexes of congregational performance, only one of which was membership growth. In roughly the same time period (1974-76) the United Presbyterian Church engaged in an extensive study of 681 "growing, typical, and rapidly declining congregations."

Both studies contain a wealth of information concerning the

churches and the communities in which they are located. The Presbyterian study includes questionnaire responses from nearly 4,000 current members and former members, and the United Church of Christ study utilizes data from over 24,000 persons attending church services in the two states. Although both denominations make use of community data, the Presbyterian study emphasizes clergy and member perception of what is happening in the community, whereas the United Church of Christ study relies on data taken from the U.S. census.

While these investigations were conducted independently and had slightly different objectives, the data collected and the nature of the analyses are quite similar. In each case it is possible to look at the relationships between church growth or decline and the characteristics of the local community and of congregational life. Fortunately, for our purposes, the number of churches included in the two studies is large enough to make possible the examination of factors related to membership within four general areas of social context: city churches, churches in stable suburban communities, churches in growing suburban communities, and town and country churches.

Remarkably similar findings resulted from the Presbyterian and the United Church of Christ studies. Some features of community and church life were consistently related to church growth, while others had little or no impact. These neutral factors often yield the most surprising information, since they challenge some of the myths many of us hold on to so dearly, and provide profiles of church growth.

The profiles are intended to be suggestive to those who minister in particular situations. They are not descriptions of specific churches or of typical congregations. They are certainly not recommended as models or ideals toward which others should strive. In several cases the suggestive nature of the material has been used as a basis for projecting implications beyond anything clearly supported by the data. Hopefully, this approach will help pastors and members to understand their own situations as being typical in some ways and unique in others. By learning more about other congregations, we may see ourselves more clearly.

## The City Church

Churches in major metropolitan areas (population over 50,000) are dominated by their social context. Church growth or decline is directly related to the available population for most mainline churches. Four contextual factors stand out as especially important in both studies:

**Socioeconomic Level of the Congregation***
**Available Protestant Population**
**Average Neighborhood Family Size**
**Racial or Ethnic Differences** (negative consequences)

Although these demographic "facts" are usually beyond the control of any particular congregation, they do have a significant impact on the way congregations respond to their situations. Many churches simply move; they leave communities in which they cannot continue an effective and self-sustaining ministry. Some rise above their circumstances by attracting regional denominational recognition.

The UCC study is especially insightful in identifying the similarities between growing congregations and the socioeconomic levels in the communities they serve. The homogeneous unit is one principle of church growth in the city. That homogeneity may be in racial/ethnic culture, socioeconomic class, or theological viewpoint. The city church must have a clear perception of itself and of its community. Without intentional clarity, the city church appears doomed by

*See appendix for correlation coefficients of membership growth with each factor listed in bold type throughout chapter 6.

changes beyond its control. The city is no place for indecision.

Studies of programming in growing city churches evoke two kinds of responses. One is very comfortable:

**Satisfaction with Worship and Program**
**Congregational Harmony and Cooperation**
**Communication and Encouragement Among Members**

A city church that is receiving new members has a significantly satisfactory congregational life and a significantly higher level of communication and mutual support among its members. The sense of satisfaction relates to the worship life of the congregation and to the great variety of programs the church is conducting. The congregation is well informed about what is happening in the church. They feel good about the activities, and they feel good about the support they receive from one another. Mutual understanding and trust seems to be more important than an agreement on theological principles. The need for trusted communication places a special burden on the pastor and on the formal and informal leadership of the city church. As one veteran said, "If the grapevine goes sour, you're dead."

The other program implication appears to be a conflict between conservative theology and social action:

**Conservative Theology**
**Organizing for the Disadvantaged**
**Community Use of Church Facilities**

Growing city congregations define their theology as conservative, using the earlier criteria previously noted in chapter 4. Yet, these churches have a significantly higher involvement in organizing for the disadvantaged and in encouraging community use of church facilities. Obviously, these effective churches found no conflict between a conserving theology and an aggressive program of social concern. They behave like mainline churches, conserving yesterday's values in the midst of today's conflicts.

A similar contradiction appears in growing churches located in older, more settled areas of the city.

**Distinctiveness from Culture**
**Church Involvement in Community Affairs**

This contrast partly reflects the regional quality of many city churches, which draw their members from a wide area and are not confined to a simple reflection of the community population. But even if their members do not reside in the neighborhood, city churches that are growing care more about their community; they are notably more involved in community affairs than congregations that are declining. One pastor suggested that the distinctiveness of his church membership was an asset to the community organization: "Many of our members no longer live in the community. We bring the perspective of outsiders and the concern of people who really care about the neighborhood."

There are also the anticipated correlations that did not occur. Contrary to those in other communities, growing churches in the city did *not* correlate with any of the following prime target groups of city population:

**Families with School-age Children**
**Percentage of Younger Persons or Older Persons in Community**
**Percentage of Home Owners/Renters in Community**

Apparently, the city churches that are growing are most effective at reaching whatever population is available. They do not require the same mix or family emphasis, which seems to characterize growing churches in suburban areas. They may not need a Sunday church school or a youth group or a disproportionate number of home owners (the homes are important, but whether they are owned or rented seems immaterial). Growing city churches "make do" with the population at hand.

Further, growing churches in the city show no inclination

toward higher levels of membership commitment. They show no significant correlation with any of the following:

**Frequency of Attending Worship**
**Contribution as a Percentage of Family Income**
**Percentage of Church Members in Church School**
**Organized Sharing of Personal Beliefs**
**Organized Recruitment for New Members**

Some growing city churches may be high-commitment congregations, but many are not. In fact, there seems to be a low-key pattern of coping, not conquering. The style of Christian witness must fit the congregation and the community.

In summary, the growing congregations in the city seem to be held together by positive communication and mutual trust, not by theological uniformity or congregational self-discipline. They report a diversified program and a steady, positive Christian witness. As active participants in the community, they reflect the mainline style of conserving and mediating Christian values.

### The Church in the Stable Suburban Community

The program patterns of growing churches in stable suburban areas appear to be similar to those of city churches—with two basic differences: first, they are significantly involved in many more activities, and second, their levels of commitment are notably higher. The following items have a positive correlation with growing congregations in stable suburbs:

**Community Use of Church Facilities**
**Satisfaction with Worship and Program**
**Congregational Harmony and Cooperation**
**Organizing for the Disadvantaged**
**Contribution as a Percentage of Family Income**
**Communication and Encouragement Among Members**
**High Membership Demands**

**Conservative Theology**
**Organized Sharing of Personal Beliefs**
**Many Small Groups and Activities**
**Advocating Social Justice**
**Organized Recruitment of New Members**
**Church Involvement in Community Affairs**

Church program contributes most to growing churches in stable suburbs. City churches are plowed under by population changes, while churches in growing suburbs depend on favorable changes in the population—both are more or less responding to their environments. In stable suburban communities, however, program is the most significant difference between growing and declining congregations.

All kinds of programs seem appropriate, with community use of church facilities heading the list of significant activities. These growing congregations show the same mainline church mix of conservative theology and advocacy for social justice, of small-group activities and widespread concern for community affairs, of organized sharing of the faith within the congregation and organized recruitment of new members from the larger community. The growing church reaches more new members with offers of more program options.

The Kelley model for church growth would seem to be especially appropriate for the mainline churches in stable suburban communities. Such congregations appear to have the level of energy and commitment that Kelley expects, yet they lack the single-minded separation from the world that he urges. Apparently, mainline churches can sustain high levels of commitment without withdrawing from the world. They are even more involved. They do it all, and they do it with gusto.

Although growing churches in stable suburbs are engaged in a large number of activities, with significantly higher levels of commitment, they still rate the social dimension of congregational life among the most important priorities. The membership's need for communication and encouragement places an even greater burden upon the pastor and the leaders. Such congregations must invest heavily in various means of communication. They must develop a first-rate newsletter and other printed materials. Further, the congregational leadership must keep the channels of communication open to accommodate the flow of positive information. Members need not agree with one another in personal faith or on congregational policies as long as they trust that the decision-making processes are available to them, that they are appreciated personally, and that the church is open to the Holy Spirit. Good process is good theology.

As for the influence of population on growth, suburban churches reflect the national profile of mainline churches. The following populations correlate with church growth in stable suburban communities:

**Families with School-age Children**
**Increase in Affluent Families**
**Young Adults**
**Increase in Families**

This pattern bears a striking resemblance to the demographic data gathered from the growing suburbs in the 1950s. They provide "our sort of people" for Protestant mainline church growth. The reverse is also true: inharmonious changes have a strong negative effect. The following items correlate positively with church decline, negatively with church growth:

**Increasing Neighborhood Population Density**
**Older Community Housing**
**Older Church Building**
**Increase of Nonresident Membership**
**Racial or Ethnic Differences**

In metropolitan areas, growing churches rise above the limitations of their social context by the ingenious development of two kinds of church participants, who might seem to be mutually exclusive: One is the *regional member,* with apparently high levels of commitment to the congregation; the other is the *community constituent member,* who shares in the activities of the church facilities without joining the congregation.

### *Regional Members*

Regional members of mainline churches come from several sources. They can be former community residents who have moved some distance from the church but who still commute for Sunday worship and for other significant activities during the week. They may be former members of another congregation that had been located in a different part of town but that moved and merged with the church to which the older members must now travel—the members have remained but the church has moved. Neither of these cases would be likely to produce the high commitment noted in growing congregations in stable communities. They are accidental, not intentional, regional members.

A positive strategy for developing regional church membership is implied in several of Walrath's types of social contextual churches. Midtown, city suburb, and independent city areas all suggest a conscious development of regional congregations: Old First, Grace Church, or Trinity Cathedral. As regional churches, they have access to resources that can maintain an especially rich mix of program offerings. They have a perspective on history that can embrace a wide range of viewpoints. They can attract the movers and shakers of the community with quality offerings, from pulpit to preschool programs. Regional churches have the opportunity to attract people from throughout the whole area who see the area as a whole, not just as communities or neighborhoods.

Regional churches do not normally reflect the population where they are located; they have other functions. They often have larger programs for young adults. They offer to the whole region a high quality of cultural events. They can reflect and challenge issues on a regional basis. In developing these unique ministries, they can often achieve a high level of membership commitment for particular program areas. Most important, they can appeal to the educated, cosmopolitan person for whom the local congregation is simply too limited. They can offer the cosmopolitan youth a Christian challenge that is big enough to match the world view they have found.

### Constituent Members

Community constituent members form the backbone of volunteer activities in many congregations. They may not be high-commitment members of the congregation as such, but they are highly committed to the activities of the congregation. Meals-on-wheels, tutoring, housing clinics, scouting programs are all dependent upon neighborhood volunteers who feel very much at home in the church building. Environmental groups, Transcendental Meditation, Parents Without Partners, and other community groups are composed of people who respond to particular needs for which the church provides space and therefore shares a concern. "Community use of church facilities" is significant for growing congregations in metropolitan areas, but it dominates the life-style of churches located in stable communities. Through community programs, congregations maintain a wide base of constituent members who feel close to the ministry of the church. These people are usually very friendly with the pastor and a few others but do not feel moved to join the congregation.

Maintaining a constituent membership is one way for mainline churches to keep in contact with those who believe without belonging. Traditional expressions of Christian faith appear inappropriate to their lives, but they work out their commitments through service and sharing in groups. To one pastor these constituents are the "program members of the congregation"; they participate by doing, not by joining. He noted that many have called on him when they needed pastoral care, when they were ill, or when their children were in trouble. After talking about his ambivalent feelings toward people who presumed upon his time without belonging to the church, he added, "I guess it's their church too, somehow."

Constituent members make two contributions: they expand the ministry of the church by working with others, and in them the church has contact with believers who do not belong. Each helps the other to be more than it was.

Regional members with high commitments and constituent members with loose commitments may appear to be opposite, even contradictory. Both find a home in the growing church in the stable community. Both are evidence of the mainline church style that seeks to mediate values throughout the region or in the intimacy of neighborhood activities.

## The Church in the Growing Suburb

The growing community makes the church grow. Mainline churches in growing communities record a higher membership growth rate than other type of congregation. But the influences for that growth are primarily related to community population changes far beyond the control of any congregation:

**Increase in Affluent Families**

**Increase in Families with School-age Children**

**Increase in Home Ownership**

**Increase in Protestant Population**

The community makes the church when "our kind of people" move in. Conversely, other social factors adversely affect church growth. The following had a negative correlation with growth and a positive relationship to decline in the suburbs:

**Age of Homes Near Church**

**Percentage of Renters**

**Increase in Minorities**

Family needs and local expenses dominate the agendas of growing congregations in new suburban communities. Much of

98

the energy of growing churches is devoted to developing programs for child care and to raising the funds to survive. Thus, the highest correlations with growth were in these areas:

**Increase in Church School Enrollment**
**Increase in Local Income and Expense**

Additional items that correlate with church growth in the growing suburb reflect the same patterns seen in other situations:

**Satisfaction with Worship and Program**
**Congregational Harmony and Cooperation**
**Organizing for the Disadvantaged**
**Community Use of Church Facilities**

In addition, two items receive unique emphasis in the growing suburban church that do not receive such significant attention elsewhere:

**Organized Recruitment of New Members**
**Many Small Groups and Church Activities**

These are interrelated dimensions of an active program to reach prospective members and to assimilate into the church those people who do join. Although committees to recruit new members are frequently recommended, only in the suburban church do they appear to be important for membership growth. Small groups are also widely endorsed as an essential part of membership assimilation and are most useful in the suburban setting.

The importance of building a firm institution is underscored by the competitive character of the task. Churches in growing suburbs are threatened by the presence of other congregations. The following conditions correlate negatively with growth, positively with church decline:

**Neighborhood Protestant Churches**
**Neighborhood Churches of the Same Denomination**
  (Presbyterian)

Growing churches in growing suburbs cannot "afford" to

engage in ecumenical activities until after the "bulge" is over and the community has settled.

Church growth in growing suburbs does not exhibit an emphasis on strong theological or personal commitments among church members. These factors were significant in growing congregations in stable suburbs, but not where church and community are growing together. No significant correlations were noted in the following areas:

**High Membership Demands**
**Organized Sharing of Personal Beliefs**
**Advocating Social Justice**
**Church Involvement in Community Affairs**
**Communication and Encouragement Among Members**

We are left with the disturbing suggestion that in growing churches in expanding suburbs—the pacesetters for the growth of mainline denominations—harmony is critical, but information is not; cooperation is important, but mutual encouragement is not.

In summary, the residual impression of a growing mainline church in a growing suburb is a congregation where children and families are the center of attention, where assimilation is through small-group activities, and where few people seem interested in knowing what the rest of the church is doing. Individual congregations may be engaged in much more, but the profile of growing suburban congregations seems centered on children and grounded in budget.

### *The Church in the Small City*

Because of the special nature of the Presbyterian study, it is possible to isolate the characteristics of growing congregations, in smaller cities, that are independent of strong metropolitan influences. The resulting profile is an interesting hybrid between the growing suburb (discussed above) and the town and country congregation (described below). In general, small cities perceive themselves as "growing." Growing churches show some characteristics similar to the church in the growing suburb. These factors are related to church growth:

**Community Use of Church Facilities**
**Satisfaction with Worship and Program**
**Organizing for the Disadvantaged**

All the correlations suggest a significantly lower level of intensity in membership. In other areas the effective church in a small city has the characteristics of the town and country congregation. For example, the following factors were important to churches in growing suburbs but are reduced to statistical insignificance for church growth in smaller cities, in striking similarity to more rural congregations. These are not statistically significant:

**Congregational Harmony and Cooperation**
**Many Small Groups and Activities**
**Organized Recruitment of New Members**

Growing churches in smaller cities seem to combine the program resources of metropolitan areas with the intimacy and family feistiness of more settled, rural communities.

### The Town and Country Church

The striking feature of the growing town and country congregation is the absence of correlations that appear to be significant in other types of communities. Notice the areas that are unrelated to growth in town and country churches:

**Congregational Harmony and Cooperation**
**Communication and Encouragement Among Members**
**Many Small Groups and Activities**
**Organized Sharing of Personal Beliefs**
**Organized Recruitment of New Members**
**Percentage of Church Members in Church School**

From this list it is apparent that the growing town and country church operates in a distinctively different organizational climate than a city or suburban congregation. Organizational structures seem to be less important to growth. Further, congregational life appears to proceed without the harmony or the encouragement that is so essential in more highly organized congregations. One might suspect that they have vested more trust in personal contact and in lifelong friendship than they have in decision-making machinery and in official church processes.

In program, the town and country congregations that are growing have a strong positive correlation with human need, community composition, and economic support of the church:

**Emphasize God's Love and Care for Each Person**
**Membership Reflects Community Composition**
**Contribution as a Percentage of Family Income**

Thus, the growing congregations in town and country areas are oriented to personal concerns, modestly responsive to demographic changes, and relatively untouched by organizational recommendations. One pastor reviewed these statistics and summarized briefly what he knew about his community: "People who are close to the soil don't need a lot of organized religion. They will always come back to the church when there is time or when there is need—whether you think they are members or not."

### The Ethnic Church

Unique characteristics of the UCC study permitted the researchers to factor out the distinctions between the more rural-based congregations of the former Evangelical and Reformed branch and the more metropolitan-oriented congregations of the Congregational Christian Churches. For example, the Congregational Christian churches increased in membership more often when the population also increased, while the former Evangelical and Reformed congregations grew in membership regardless of changes in the general

102

population. Membership growth in former Evangelical and Reformed congregations is related to their greater emphasis upon family ties, to the larger size of Evangelical and Reformed families, and to their extended participation in the church school. In short, Evangelical and Reformed families produce their own members and keep them more involved in the life of the church. Similar comments have also been made about the growth of the Southern Baptist Convention (see chapter 4).

Former Evangelical and Reformed congregations, with their German ethnic heritage, serve as a very general prototype for a great array of ethnic congregations in America. Such churches typically place more emphasis on God's love and concern for each member and less importance on the involvement of the church in social action issues. Within these extended family congregations, the dominant theology is personal caring and corporate conserving of basic Christian values. In fact, formerly Evangelical and Reformed congregations, more so than formerly Congregational Christian congregations, are likely to express their dissatisfaction when the conditions conspire to produce too many new members. William J. McKinney has suggested that this dissatisfaction might be due to the "disruptive effect of membership growth on existing members and their relationship with 'their' church."

With such familiar characteristics, ethnic congregations must be noted as a distinctively different kind of congregation, which is not as directly dependent upon the population of a specific geographic base. Ethnic congregations are another sort of regional church.

In this chapter we have seen that effective churches grow in relation to the contextual potential of the communities where they are located. These profiles are not intended to prescribe program or to inhibit experimentation. By identifying characteristics of effective and growing congregations, not in general but as found in more specific kinds of communities, we have tried to liberate the pastor and the congregation from the tyranny of inappropriate expectations or of nationally prescribed programs. By looking at other situations that are more like our own, we hope to know more about ourselves and about the ways that others like us have brought the faith alive.

# CHAPTER 7

# Leadership: A Good Word for Pastors

The importance of the pastor in the growth and decline of mainline congregations has been reserved until last because it remains especially controversial. One group of analysts has made the pastor the pivotal person around which to build a growing congregation. Another group has suggested that the pastor makes important but specific contributions within the limits of growth established by other factors.

The church growth movement in general and the particular 188th General Assembly (1976) Report on United Presbyterian Church Membership Trends located the pastor in the primary position. By using case studies of successful churches and denominational inclinations, the key has been identified: growth depends upon the pastor. Accordingly, the pastor must be well prepared, deeply committed, hardworking, clear in vision, and capable of arousing enthusiasm in the congregation; others have added "able to walk on water and, especially, to raise the dead."

Gifted pastors have accomplished miracles, by the grace of God, in reviving congregations that had shown no vital signs and were presumed dead. When churches come alive, the pastor also is empowered. He or she reflects the prayers and trust that have been bestowed by a responsive congregation.

105

The people of a revitalized church often make the pastor look good and feel well. If the chemistry is right, the pastor and the people fit together in a growing congregation.

Case studies, especially in superchurches and in growing communities, can be misleading, and negative comparisons can be demoralizing. We have access to studies of mainline churches that are both growing and declining, located in a cross section of communities to avoid a bias toward more advantageous areas. In these studies, the charisma of the pastor does not dominate. The most gifted pastors can be captive to unworkable conditions. The most promising congregations can be frustrated by inappropriate leadership. These studies suggest five areas in which pastors make a significant contribution to church growth.

### Believing in the Church

The pastor's attitude and approach to the congregation permeates every study of congregational growth and decline. Enthusiasm is a key contribution to worship, and confidence is supportive for church program development. Although professional competence is not unimportant, skills do not make the impact that attitude does. Membership satisfaction in worship and program has the strongest correlation with numerical growth or decline. The most consistent contribution to program satisfaction is the attitude of the pastor.

In the church growth movement, Peter Wagner has lifted this attitude to the skill of "possibility thinking." That is, the pastor contributes imagination and positive alternatives to the previously limited vision of the congregational or church group. Clark Roof has doubts if such an exotic description is accurate for the typical pastor of a growing mainline congregation. However, both agree that the pastor's energetic and enthusiastic support of church ministry has a strong positive correlation with the appeal for and assimilation of new members into a growing church.

Some pastors of mainline churches have confused the prophetic role of mediating the faith with a kind of permeating negativism about either the purity of the church or the health of the society. The prophetic word in the 1960s was often seen by members as negative thinking without a positive alternative. After a particularly disturbing sermon about racism in the church, one devout parishioner was heard to whisper, "The young man doubts God and trusts the government. He has it backwards!" Such a misunderstanding of the prophetic role of the church is apparently incompatible with growth in mainline congregations.

Enthusiasm has many effects upon the pastor and the congregation. Attitude can be contagious, with positive results through the congregation and in the community. Enthusiasm can be exhausting for the pastor who feels that no one else shares his dream for the church or her vision of the future. Enthusiasm can become a performance, a painted smile, when emotions lack roots in personal Christian conviction or lack support from at least a few others who see beyond the immediate problem. A pastor who no longer believes in the continuing ministry of a particular congregation may be a barrier to the work of the Spirit in that church. There are exceptions, when grave doubts about particular congregations should be voiced openly. But, in general, a pastor should be genuinely enthusiastic about the congregation's current and continuing ministry. If this is not possible, the pastor should prayerfully consider seeking a call to another church. A similar question should be put to the layperson who is beset by doubts, fears, and negative expectations. A church cannot hope to be effective when believers no longer expect God to work through their ministry. Attitude is of first importance.

### *Pastoral Care*

Pastoral care in mainline churches moves far beyond the responsibilities of the pastor to care for confessional members of the congregation. Mainline pastors are often invited to pray at public events and to provide chaplain services to organizations that include members of other faiths and people who make no confession of faith. These symbolic acts suggest that pastors are concerned for more than their own members and that the church they serve is concerned for the people of the community. Many times these positions of public recognition, along with the presence of the pastor in many community activities, provide an invitation for nonmembers throughout the community who have a personal need or a family crisis.

Believers who do not belong frequently turn to the institutional forms of religion in times of crisis. When they are seriously ill or when someone close to them is hospitalized, they may reach for the reassurance symbolized in the person of the pastor. When they are threatened by job loss or court action, they may turn to the friendlier structures of the church. When they greet the mystery of life in a newborn child or the mystery of love between two adults or the mystery of separation in death, they may turn to the church and ask the pastor to walk with them through the valley.

Mainline pastors who have made themselves available to the community are constantly being asked to share the lives of church members and of believers who do not belong. Both confessional and constituent members of the congregation make their requests for help with a mixture of signals. Sometimes they make a straightforward request or a simple statement of need, to see if the pastor (or church member) is listening. Other times they criticize the church (in apparently irrelevant areas), overwork in some church activity, or withdraw from habitual participation—all forms of asking for attention.

New Believers test the sincerity of pastoral care in two ways: Will the church stand with me in the crisis of transition, even though I am not an "official" member? Will the church pressure me to join after the crisis has passed? The first is a question of responsiveness: Will the church respond to need? The second is a question of integrity: Does the church really respect the integrity of my separateness? Some pastors respond to need but hope the debt will be paid when the person subsequently joins the congregation. Other pastors and congregations are proud to render the service, "freely given in Jesus' name."

Mainline faith invites but never demands church membership. Pastoral care for mainline churches involves both the pastor and the congregation in services for which there is no return on investment, at least not on earth. It takes a special kind of faith to allow the constituent member the right not to join the congregation, without breaking the ties that hold each together in the community of belief and ministry. Membership is, after all, the work of the Spirit, not an achievement of the pastor or the congregation.

### *Faith in the Middle*

Mainline churches have taken a mediating position in the middle of the culture. Growing congregations conserve the values of the past, engage the community in areas of common concern, and share their buildings for all manner of character development and Christian witness. The behavior of mainline churches reaffirms the assumption of their faith. The burden of the pastor is to clarify the faith that is implicit in mainline church programs.

The theological task of the mainline pastor is to affirm the necessity for personal faith in Jesus Christ, for congregational and denominational diversity in the ways that faith is understood, and for religious pluralism in the public arena. The pastor must be clear that this combination of private faith and public pluralism is not a compromise, negotiated in weakness when truth failed to triumph over falsehood. Mainline churches must find strength in the pluralism to which critics have pointed as a weakness.

Fundamentalists, neo-evangelicals, suburban elitists, right- and left-wing political radicals are always momentarily "stronger" than mainline churches. They have screened out differences and can proclaim a unity of belief, a commitment of the true believers to a single perspective for everyone. As sectarian slices of the total culture, they will always present a more united front.

Mainline theology has upheld their freedom to speak and to be heard. Mainline Christians have listened in search of new revelation. Mainline church members have been tempted by some views and threatened by others. Americans are constantly tempted to find a clear alternative to the ambiguity and uncertainty that plagues those who listen to many perspectives in an effort to see the whole. But this religious pluralism lies at the very heart of the mainline Protestant church enterprise. It is entirely logical for UCGD to contain a variety of viewpoints, including several strongly sectarian statements, that do not agree with one another. That is the strength, not the weakness, of the Protestant tradition.

Mainline pastoral leadership is called upon to affirm the strength of pluralism in two seemingly opposite ways: as an advocate for a particular faith and as a protector for the rights of those who disagree. People with strong sectarian viewpoints might consider the tension impossible. But for the mainline pastor, neither faith nor pluralism can exist without the other. The pastor is called to help mainline church members understand why pluralism is affirmed in the center of the culture, and not from the sidelines.

### Good Management

Good management is more than the efficient organization of church groups or the careful supervision of resources and personnel. Good management is the development of a common vision, a ministry that the congregation accepts, supports, and enjoys.

Two dimensions of good management are essential in mainline churches: one positive and the other negative. On the positive side, growing congregations are more apt to be doing more things, to know more about what they are doing, and to feel good about it. The pastor is pivotal in helping the congregation to grasp a vision of their ministry and to appreciate the values of their diversities. The process of helping the congregation to appreciate itself appears to be much more important, and more difficult, in the pluralism of mainline churches than in congregations where prescribed theology or authoritarian leadership determines acceptable program and beliefs. In mainline churches, polity is a theology because it permits religious pluralism. There is some truth to what the church parliamentarian claims: "The Book of Order (or discipline) is my Bible."

On the negative side, controversy—especially in the mismanagement of social action issues—is frequently associated with membership decline. Yet, social concerns are, of themselves, positively related to growth. Growing congregations are more apt to be concerned for the disadvantaged, to be involved in community issues, and to invite community groups to use the church facilities. Growing churches are involved; declining churches fight about involvement.

Controversies over social issues can be caused by several factors. The congregation can be divided beyond the limits of logical tolerance, so that the members cannot hear one another. Controversy can be evoked by a closed process, through the manipulation of a militant minority of the congregation or the personal need of the pastor. The congregation can simply lack a compelling vision of a mainline church seeking to mediate the grace of God to the wholeness of society. Good management finds a way to resolve internal conflict so that members ap-

111

preciate how much they need one another for the sake of their common faith and ministry. Unity of purpose and mutual appreciation rate far more heavily with growing churches than any measure of theological conformity or religious intolerance. Good management is good theology in mainline churches.

## *Personal Faith*

The faith of the pastor is evident, not just because of his function as the organizer and the theologian of the congregation, but even more so in his role as the concerned Christian who shares in love with those of the congregation and the community. Two examples may be drawn from UCGD.

First, pastors are significantly and universally involved in helping members of growing congregations see ways in which they could take their ministries into the world around them. Of all the areas of ministry in the congregations studied, effective pastors are most frequently associated with their congregations' concerns for the social needs of people in the communities where they live and through the ministry of the denomination around the world. Pastors may be instrumental in bringing in new members, raising more funds, inspiring biblical insights, or effecting efficient organizational management, but in growing mainline congregations they are uniquely identified with helping the congregation to define its faith and carry out that vision in its ministry to the community.

Second, pastors are important as people who make themselves available when they are needed. Without being pretentious, they accept the personal priestly function of their office. Because they are held by a faith in the love of God, they are willing to share the pain of members of the parish, to be vulnerable to their anger, and to be shaken by their anguish. Aware of sinful humanity, imperfect institutions, and the constant need for God's sustaining grace, they are relatively free of personal needs to dominate when other people need

112

them. They reclaim the priestly tradition of mainline Reformation churches: each is a priest to all others, and everyone needs a priest at one time or another. In faith they are willing to share the human experience. As Christians they recount the divine intervention.

In growing churches the faith of the minister is important. He or she is seen as someone close to God and close to the people. Faith needs no apology and no coercion.

### Independent Identity

The theological skepticism and anti-institutional orientation of New Believers who feel no need to belong has pushed the pastor one step closer to identifying with the community. Previously, pastors allowed their community participation to develop directly from their responsibilities as leaders of a religious institution. As long as the church was held in high regard, their leadership in the community seemed to follow naturally. But the New Believers are skeptical about hidden motives and institutional self-interest associated with religious leadership in secular affairs.

Many pastors working in communities of New Believers have developed an independent identity in the community. This new status is an expression of personal concern as a Christian and as a citizen, not as a pastor of a local congregation. In some situations this independent position has provided supplementary income, a tentmaking ministry in the fashion of the apostle Paul (Acts 18:3). Other positions develop as a unique match of the pastor's interests and the community's needs. Pastors have served as community developers, paramedics, part-time teachers, local political party leaders, and so on.

The independent identity of the pastor provides a bridge to many people who believe but cannot belong to the church for a variety of reasons. At the same time, it can easily be misunderstood by church leaders in the congregation and in denominational offices. Although these community responsibilities for the pastor may grow spontaneously in response to need, they should be clarified by the pastor with the groups to whom the pastor is accountable. Many clergy have found a written contract helpful to specify the nature of the work, the time involved, and the compensation received, if any. The initiative for establishing the contract rests with the minister, who needs the understanding and prayerful support of the church as a prerequisite for a believable, independent identity in the community.

In summary, the pastor is very important in mainline congregations that have proven themselves effective witnesses for Christ. The profile of an effective pastor is neither up front nor in the spotlight. Extraordinary gifts and boundless energy are not the features necessarily associated with pastors in a cross section of growing congregations.

Effective pastors are not passive in their leadership. They project an image of enthusiasm, pluralism, hope, personal faith, and independent identity. They are believable Christians. They work in and through the congregation, not expecting to do it all themselves. They are well aware, as shepherds of their flocks, that most sheep do not follow the shepherd, but follow other sheep. They provide good leadership, not as a stellar activity, but as a faithful servant in the whole community.

Leadership is a good word for pastors and a blessing to the churches they serve. The difference is not technical knowlege but positive faith.

# CHAPTER 8

# *Facts, Faith, and Strategy*

The continued decline of church membership in mainline denominations threatens their standings among the churches of the nation and challenges the imagination of denominational leadership. The information is not new, but the accumulation of so many studies that point in a similar direction forces us to take a new look at what we may have known only unconsciously. Behind the mass of data looms the shadow of an apparent shift in values among the population that has been the source of membership for mainline churches. If mainline Protestant churches are to survive, they must make substantial adjustments to meet the new situation.

The evidence of declining church membership is indisputable, but the causes for lost membership are not as clear, since there is no single path by which we can trace the departure. These lost members have not trooped off en masse to join other denominations or religious groups, and they do not seem to be angry with the church as such. Without defining all the causes, we can identify a massive shift of cultural values during the 1960s. The largest number of lost members is associated with the rising religious affirmation of New Believers.

New Believers tend to be graduates of the middle-class ladder of success. They have internalized their beliefs and have sacrificed home ties for higher education and greater economic mobility. They have emphasized personal freedom, individual decisions, and private religious experience. They believe without belonging.

An increase in the number of New Believers has triggered a variety of reactions among church leaders:

Some have vigorously denied that the change of values has caused the membership decline. They have other theories, based on their own experience and research. Since other denominations have increased while mainline denominations have declined, they claim that the cause for the losses must be found within the policies, programs, and personnel of mainline church organization.

Anger is sometimes elicited by the suggestion that declining membership is caused by changing values over which the church has no direct control. While some people react emotionally, others intimate that this may be an attempt to protect incompetent or uncommitted leadership.

A necessary first step in using this material is to honestly admit that the church must minister to the world as it finds it. As the contextual factors in this study unfold, it comes as a shock to some and a comfort to others to realize how little any person or group can do to avert the storms of history or the tides of changing cultural values. So much is beyond our control that we should feel liberated from undue pride or inappropriate guilt.

Some church leaders have confirmed their awareness of the New Believers with a kind of welcome resignation. For them, the designation of New Believers provides an explanation for their present situation. Sometimes they empathize with the anti-institutional attitudes of those who believe but do not belong. Rather than fight, they seem ready to switch.

There is no reason for their resignation. Taken as a problem in marketing research, the New Believer is only one of several populations available for church growth. With these studies we can identify, in general, what works with which population.

Denominations can target homogeneous and heterogeneous communities with some indexes of initial costs and potential results. Program materials can be sized for congregations, and congregations can be styled to reach particular populations. Denominations can deploy resources with a relatively accurate prediction of return on investment. We are not helpless within the limits of communities chosen and methods employed. And miracles are always welcome.

However, the analogy of market analysis sharpens the issue for mainline Protestants. The swelling ranks of New Believers draw their numbers from the population that once provided members to mainline churches. These New Believers are not opposed to organized religion for other people; they just do not want it themselves. For the sake of survival, old mainline churches must either find a new source of members or a way of relating to old members.

## Denominational Decisions

Typically, growing congregations have a greater clarity about themselves and a greater affinity for the cultural group they are trying to reach. In their sharpest forms, Strong Churches demand theological conformity and Cultural Churches concentrate on ethnoeconomic enclaves. They make the most of the fractured character of our communities and the polarized loyalties of our society. They are exclusive in membership and are withdrawn from the public arena. They are churches that grow!

Mainline denominational church policies are caught among three imperatives: They must retain sufficient continuity with the past so that they do not confuse and lose the commitment of their present membership. Yet, they must move toward greater clarity of purpose and sharper focus on a single population to accelerate their membership appeal. But by choosing the clarity of a sectarian community, mainline congregations tend to alienate themselves from the great mass of New Believers.

In the practice of ministry, effective mainline denominations remain what they have always been: not either/or, but both/and. Some congregations will affirm the principles of Strong Churches; some will follow the line of Cultural Christians. Most congregations will have groups that do some of both, and much more. They will conserve the values of the past, seek justice for the oppressed, and provide care for those in need. They will continue as mediators of Christian values in the midst of cultural diversity.

Denominational organization makes possible the mainline heritage in two ways: First, the denominations carry mainline traditions from Europe and from all their contributions in American history. Second, they provide an arena that is large enough for developing resources and diverse enough for gathering a vision of the churches together that none can gain alone. Denominations can provide the place and the process for radically different viewpoints to be joined in a common cause or can share their resources for their different needs.

In times as divided as ours, the burden of conflict is often shifted from the congregation to the denominational structure. We might measure the effectiveness of a denomination, not by its own achievements, but by the diversity of elements it is able to embrace, each doing its own thing, together.

### *Congregational Strategy*

The continued witness of mainline denominations, perhaps their survival as well, depends upon how much the ministry of confessional members can be expanded to embrace the outsiders, the constituent members. As membership rolls of mainline churches decline, the involvement and support of local constituencies must increase to make up the difference.

Membership definitions may become flexible in many

effective congregations. They designate New Believers who share in ministry as "friends of the church," "kindred spirits," or "covenant-seekers." Such a flexible understanding of membership poses a major problem for Strong Churches and is perhaps too easily accommodated in Cultural Churches. Each must find an appropriate way, but a way must be found.

Programs of effective congregations raise up areas of common concern to both confessional members and local constituents of New Believers, such as caring for the earth or sharing spiritual growth, neighborhood improvement or community mental health. In order to give focus and to expand participation in the rhythm of community experience, community celebrations are included as part of worship. The church school projects an expanded image that includes but is larger than the nuclear family. The pace of group life allows for easy access without demanding permanent commitments. Effective mainline congregations assume the legitimacy of faith in the New Believers and seek ways for each to participate on her or his own terms.

In the same way, the pastor is not a captive to the institutional church, but has a presence in the community as a religious leader and also as a human being concerned about the welfare of others. To reach the New Believer, the pastor must be a person concerned for others in tasks that stand apart from the needs of organized religion.

The advent of the New Believer forces the mainline Protestant churches to make an old decision new: Will they remain faithful to their heritage, mediating Christian values, even when the task is unprofitable and the future unpredictable? The New Believer, who feels no need to belong, precipitates basic changes in the patterns of mainline Christian witness in America. Either the ministry will be shared with others or mainline churches will withdraw to the sidelines. The New Believer has arrived; the next move belongs to the churches.

119

# *Factors Affecting Church Membership Growth by Type of Community*

(Compiled by John E. Dyble)

## *Large Cities*

*Contextual Factors:*

| | |
|---|---|
| Socioeconomic Level of the Congregation | .27 |
| | .22* |
| Available Protestant Population | .23 |
| Average Neighborhood Family Size | .26* |

*Negative Contextual Factor:*

| | |
|---|---|
| Racial or Ethnic Differences | −.27 |
| | −.22* |

*Church Program Factors:*

| | |
|---|---|
| Satisfaction with Worship and Program | |
| —in both growing and nongrowing areas | .24 |

*Indicates correlation is from the United Church of Christ study (UCGD, chap. 10). All others are from the United Presbyterian study (UCGD, chap. 9). Correlations for church program factors in the United Presbyterian study were computed after controlling for community affluence and demographic change.

Distinctiveness from Culture
  —in growing areas                                      .01
  —in nongrowing areas                                   .24
Congregational Harmony and Cooperation
  —in growing areas                                      .21
  —in nongrowing areas                                   .33
Communication and Encouragement Among
    Members
  —in growing areas                                      .14
  —in nongrowing areas                                   .27
Conservative Theology
  —in growing areas                                      .21
  —in nongrowing areas                                   .14
Organizing for the Disadvantaged
  —in growing areas                                      .09
  —in nongrowing areas                                   .21
Church Involvement in Community Affairs
  —in growing areas                                      .05
  —in nongrowing areas                                   .14
Community Use of Church Facilities
  —in both growing and nongrowing areas                  .12
Many Small Groups and Activities
  —in both growing and nongrowing areas                  .09

*Neutral Factors:*
  Percentage of Families in Neighborhood
  Families with School-age Children
  Percentage of Younger Persons in Community
  Percentage of Older Persons in Community
  Percentage of Home Owners/Renters in
      Community
  Percentage of Church Members in Church School*
  Frequency of Attending Worship*
  Contribution as a Percentage of Family Income*
  Organized Sharing of Personal Beliefs
  Organized Recruitment for New Members

## Suburban Areas with Stable Populations

*Contextual Factors:*

| | |
|---|---|
| Families with School-age Children | .33 |
| Increase in Affluent Families | .28 |
| Young Adults | .18 |
| Increase in Families | .19 |

*Negative Contextual Factors:*

| | |
|---|---|
| Increasing Neighborhood Population Density | −.54* |
| Older Community Housing | −.36 |
| Older Church Building | −.23 |
| Increase of Nonresident Members | −.25* |
| Racial or Ethnic Differences | −.22* |

*Church Program Factors:*

| | |
|---|---|
| Community Use of Church Facilities | .44 |
| Satisfaction with Worship and Program | .40 |
| Congregational Harmony and Cooperation | .30 |
| Organizing for the Disadvantaged | .28 |
| Contribution as a Percentage of Family Income | .28* |
| Communication and Encouragement Among Members | .22 |
| High Membership Demands | .20 |
| Conservative Theology | .18 |
| Organized Sharing of Personal Beliefs | .17 |
| Many Small Groups and Activities | .17 |
| Advocating Social Justice | .16 |
| Organized Recruitment of New Members | .10 |
| Church Involvement in Community Affairs | .10 |

## Suburban Areas with Growing Populations

*Contextual Factors:*

| | |
|---|---|
| Increase in Affluent Families | .41 |
| Increase in Families with School-age Children | .34 |

| | |
|---|---|
| Increase in Home Ownership | .23* |
| Increase in Protestant Population | .20 |

*Negative Contextual Factors:*

| | |
|---|---|
| Neighborhood Protestant Churches | −.37 |
| Neighborhood Churches of Same Denomination (Presbyterian) | −.27 |
| Age of Homes Near Church | −.30 |
| Percentage of Renters | −.21 |
| Increase in Minorities | −.19 |

*Church Program Factors:*

| | |
|---|---|
| Increase in Church School Enrollment | .33 |
| Increase in Local Income and Expenses | .30 |
| Satisfaction with Worship and Program | .24 |
| Congregational Harmony and Cooperation | .20 |
| Many Small Groups and Activities | .20 |
| Organizing for the Disadvantaged | .19 |
| Community Use of Church Facilities | .17 |
| Organized Recruitment of New Members | .10 |

*Neutral Factors:*

High Membership Demands
Organized Sharing of Personal Beliefs
Advocating Social Justice
Church Involvement in Community Affairs
Communication and Encouragement Among
    Members

## *Small Cities*

*Church Program Factors:*

| | |
|---|---|
| Community Use of Church Facilities | .16 |
| Satisfaction with Worship and Program | .15 |
| Organizing for the Disadvantaged | .15 |

*Neutral Factors:*
  Congregational Harmony and Cooperation
  Many Small Groups and Activities
  Organized Recruitment of New Members

## *Town and Country*

*Contextual Factors:*
  Percentage of Renters in Community               .14
  Increase of Young Adults                         .15

*Negative Contextual Factor:*
  Increase of Older Persons in Community (decrease
    of youth)                                     −.13

*Church Program Factors:*
  Emphasize God's Love and Care for Each Person    .26*
  Contribution as a Percentage of Family Income    .20*
  Membership Reflects Community Composition        .18*

*Neutral Factors:*
  Congregational Harmony and Cooperation
  Communication and Encouragement Among
    Members
  Many Small Groups and Activities
  Organized Sharing of Personal Beliefs
  Organized Recruitment of New Members
  Percentage of Church Members in Church School*

# Worksheets for Church Groups

Materials for meditation, discussion, and further reading.

### Chapter 1    Believing Without Belonging

**For Bible Study:**

For church members, believing and belonging may seem inseparable: religious people would join the church. Yet, in the Gospel of John, which places the most emphasis upon One Flock, there is room for unrecognized believers. Study the passages where Jesus speaks of believers who are beyond the fellowship of the disciples: John 6:35-39, 10:11-16, 11:45-52, and 12:30-32.

**For Group Discussion:**

*Church membership trends.*    Individuals enter this study from many different perspectives. Some people have never experienced a declining congregation and others cannot remember when the membership was increasing. Many others have not considered the issue, either the facts of membership change or the feelings that accompany such changes. The study group might begin by sharing personal experiences and feelings about church growth and decline. For further reading in UCGD, see the Foreword and chapters 1 and 6.

*Unusable answers.*    Most church leaders have pet theories for the recent membership losses in mainline churches. However, it is disruptive for the group to discuss these theories before they have been introduced into the text in subsequent chapters. Research in UCGD explores these theories from two

125

perspectives on two levels: the reports look at environmental conditions (social context), over which the churches have very little influence, and at church decisions (institutional factors). Both contextual and institutional factors are examined on the national and the local level. Wealth, for example, is considered in chapters 2, 4-5, 8, 14-15 of UCGD. The impact of church involvement in social issues is considered in chapters 4 and 8-10. Most issues are considered from several perspectives.

*New Believers.*   Do members of the group recognize anyone who might be considered a New Believer? Do you consider them to be Christian? or religious? or not really a believer at all? Have you shared in the four areas of faith emphasis—personal experience, spiritual growth, anti-institutionalism, and human community? Resources in UCGD: chapters 1-4 and 14.

*Mainline church dilemma.*   The importance we place on the New Believer seems to determine how we anticipate the future. Some people suggest that we need to keep on doing what we have been doing only try a little harder. Others suggest that we must respond to a new situation. Do we need to reach the New Believer? If so, how? In UCGD, Dean Kelley, Lyle Schaller, and Peter Wagner urge more effort, while Robert Evans, Dean Hoge, and James Smylie encourage a shift of emphasis.

**For Further Reading in This Area**

Charles Y. Glock and Robert N. Bellah, eds., *The New Religious Consciousness.* Berkeley: University of California Press, 1976.

Martin E. Marty, *A Nation of Behavers.* Chicago: University of Chicago Press, 1976.

### *Chapter 2   Portable, Affordable Religion*

**For Bible Study:**

The study of the rich young ruler (Matthew 19:16-30 and Mark 10:17-31) contains all the elements of the American Dream: faith, career, family, and individual fulfillment. Yet, the emphasis is distinctly Christian. The story offers a contrast to the forces discussed in chapter 2 and perhaps an explanation for chapter 3.

## For Group Discussion:

*The American Dream.* Church membership has been shown to correlate with the affirmation of religious belief, church commitment, nuclear family, and individual fulfillment. Are these values biblical? Are they basically Christian? Are there priorities among these values? Resources in UCGD: chapters 2-4.

*Suburban strategy.* Was the suburban emphasis upon new church development necessary at the time? Is it necessary now? What is the effect of seeking "our sort of people"? Is the homogeneous unit a necessary principle of church growth? Is it biblical? Resources in UCGD: chapters 2-3 and 9-13.

*Mobility as a mind-set.* How has mobility affected your congregation in its membership, in its lay leadership, and in its pastoral continuity? Lyle Schaller has suggested that a conflict may exist between the early pioneers and the later settlers: is that true for your church? How do you help members assimilate into the congregation? How do you help them to move on? Resources in UCGD: chapters 2, 8, 11, and 16.

*Affordable faith.* Dean Kelley calls for denominational programs that strengthen churches through loyalty, solidarity, zeal, distinctiveness, and discipline. In what kinds of churches are these programs most effective? Would they be helpful in your congregation? Dean Hoge has noted that the denominations where these disciplines are most effective have lower family incomes and tend to stand apart from the American Dream. Would these findings mirror your experience? Resources in UCGD: chapters 3, 8, 13, and 15.

## For Further Reading in This Area:

Rodney Stark and Charles Y. Glock, *American Piety: The*

*Nature of the Religious Commitment.* Los Angeles: University of California Press, 1968.

Gibson Winter, *The Suburban Captivity of the Churches.* New York: Macmillan, 1962.

## Chapter 3    Where Have All Our People Gone?

**For Bible Study:**

Paul used the religious base of Greek culture as a common foundation to proclaim the Christian gospel. Study Acts 17:22-34. In what ways do the Athenians sound like first-century New Believers? Would Paul have been able to reach them if they had accepted the resurrection but rejected the church? What is the best approach to the New Believers?

**For Group Discussion:**

*Family life cycle.*    This position has been most succinctly stated by Widick Schroeder in "Age Cohorts, the Family Life Cycle, and Participation in the Voluntary Church in America: Implications for Membership Patterns, 1950-2000" (*Chicago Theological Seminary Register,* 65:13-28 [1975]). Most mainline churches have made heavy commitments to the family life cycle in the construction of substantial educational facilities. Are young parents joining your congregation? Are the young leaders able to replace the loss of the elderly? Most mainline congregations are "growing older." Is yours? Resources in UCGD: chapters 2, 5-6, 14, and 16.

*Values in conflict.*    Most church members seem to recognize these values even in the conflicts they have had within the family or among close friends. Some of these conflicts are too personal for easy group discussion. In appreciation of the sensitive nature of the material, the group may have difficulty sharing experiences of conflicting values as suggested in this section. Have these Young Believers abandoned the faith or simply applied it more individually? Resources in UCGD:

chapters 2, 4, 11, and 14, with an opposite view strongly stated in chapter 15.

*Young Believers.* Some church members have claimed that the Young Believers have made the faith not only portable, but pliable to fit any situation. Do you see Young Believers as secularists? humanists? rationalists? Or do you see them as being even more self-centered? as happy hedonists? lazy Christians and lightweight materialists? What kinds of commitments are necessary and essential for salvation? If there is a rift between members and Young Believers, can a common ground be found? Resources in UCGD: chapters 2, 4–5, and 13-16.

### For Further Reading in This Area:

Dean R. Hoge, *Commitment on Campus: Changes in Religion and Values Over Five Decades.* Philadelphia: Westminster Press, 1974.

Robert Wuthnow, *The Consciousness Reformation.* Berkeley: University of California Press, 1976.

## *Chapter 4    Choices for Churches*

### For Bible Study:

Pentecost (Acts 2) is the birthday of the church. No single approach or theological "ism" has a monopoly on the meaning of this passage. Our evangelism must reflect the full dimensions of this event, from the gift of the Spirit to the explanation of the incarnate Word, from the gathering of many tongues (yet each hearing "in his own language," v. 6) to the sharing of many resources. Do these elements guide our choices? Is there one way or several?

### For Group Discussion:

In order to deal most directly with the choices that face churches, the group might begin by listing the environmental factors (social context) over which the church has very little control yet which directly affect the growth and decline of churches. Within certain broad limits, church decisions do make a difference.

*Strong Christian churches.* When do people need the greatest clarity of religious answers? We have previously touched on the Kelley thesis, noting the specific correlation between more disciplined churches and lower socioeconomic populations (chapter 2 above). Can the Kelley thesis be broadened to include others who are spiritually hungry and in need of healing for body, mind, and soul? Does the strictness of community appeal more at particular periods of our lives and in particular settings? Is it appropriate only for certain people and not for everyone? Is the Kelley thesis the most "Christian" approach? Resources in UCGD: compare chapter 15 with chapters 2-4, 8-14, and passim.

*Cultural Christian churches.* Do groups of homogeneous peoples feel more comfortable with their feelings? with expressing their Christian faith? We have previously considered the principles of the church growth movement (chapter 2), noting the almost universal sociological evidence that membership growth is more evident among homogeneous populations. Does the evidence of growth prove that the process is Christian and is blessed by God? How do you decide if a church is a Christian congregation? Did Kelley make it too difficult to become a Christian? Has Wagner made it too easy? Why does the Kelley thesis seem to be most effective in stable and declining communities, while the Wagner approach seems more akin to churches in growing suburbs? Resources in UCGD: compare chapter 12 with chapters 2, 4, and 8-14.

*Exceptional growth:* For further information see the fascinating study by Phillip Jones (UCGD, chap. 7).

*Mediating Christian values:* Why do mainline churches make social pronouncements? What do members of your group believe is the effect of social witness upon membership growth and decline in mainline denominations? Do members agree with the stands taken by the church? Do they believe that the church should be involved? Studies in UCGD show a correlation which suggests that growing mainline churches are both conservative and involved in social witness. Is that your experience? Is it biblical? Resources in UCGD: research in chapters 8-11. Note the contrast in interpretation between James Smylie, Dean Hoge, and Dean Kelley; between Robert Evans and Peter Wagner.

*Low middle ground.* Compare the foreword by Martin Marty with the data regarding the West Coast in chapters 2 and 8 in UCGD.

*The choice of a future.* How much choice do mainline churches have? Can they embrace the Kelley principles or avoid the Wagner realities? Can mainline churches bridge the New Believers' lack of commitment without losing the commitment of their current membership? What different approaches will be necessary to reach the New Believers?

**For Further Reading in This Area:**

Dean R. Hoge, *Division in the Protestant House: The Basic Reasons Behind Intra-Church Conflicts.* Philadelphia: Westminster Press, 1976.

Dean M. Kelley, *Why Conservative Churches Are Growing.* New York: Harper & Row, 1972.

Martin E. Marty, *The Righteous Empire: The Protestant Experience in America.* New York: Dial Press, 1970.

C. Peter Wagner, *Your Church Can Grow: Seven Signs of a Healthy Church.* Glendale, CA: Regal Books, 1976.


## *Chapter 5    Programming to Include the Outsider*

**For Bible Study:**

Just as Jesus died for the believers who were unknown to the disciples (John 10:16), in the same way the apostle Paul lives to reach those who are within the law and those who are outside the law. Study 1 Corinthians 9:19-23, looking for implications in the development of church programs to hold those who care for the church and to reach those who do not. Was it easy for Paul? Will it be easier for us?

**For Group Discussion:**

*Worship.* For members, what are the most appealing aspects of your worship? Are these the same for visitors? Can you identify the "audiences" in your congregation? Is something for each included in worship? What are the sources of conflict in worship? What are the satisfactions? What are the celebrations to bring in the outsiders? Resources in UCGD: chapters 2, 9, 13-14.

*The church school.* Is the emphasis upon children or adults in church school? Does that emphasis reflect the future? Does the church school reflect the changing patterns of family life in the congregation and community? Does it include nonmember children? adults? families? Resources in UCGD: chapters 2, 5-6, 14, 16.

*Small groups.* Here are some criteria for diversity in small groups: Are some open and some closed, some for new members and some for old associates? Are some groups for physical activities, such as church maintenance and recreation, while other groups are for study, reflection, and prayer? Are some groups temporary, even for one meeting, one weekend, one common project? Resources in UCGD: chapters 8-10, 12-14, 16.

*Dropouts.* For many congregations, dropouts are the first concern of an evangelism committee. From the current research they would appear to be more likely candidates for pastoral care. Who helps the pastor listen and respond to the broken relationships? Resources in UCGD: chapters 2 and 16.

*Organizing for new members.* Does the recruitment-evangelism committee conceal a problem of a changing church community or a congregation that lacks enthusiasm? Effective committees seem to boost the enthusiasm of the congregation, not provide an alternative. Resources in UCGD: chapters 2, 9, and 16.

*Local church leadership.* Can you identify the unofficial leaders of the congregation (those with financial clout are usually concerned with single issues, those with the old grapevine are often more concerned with style, tradition, and appropriate recognition)? How do the official and unofficial leaders work together? Who makes sure that the outsider is included? Resources in UCGD: chapters 9-10, 12, and 14.

*Denominational policies.* What are the most appropriate decisions for denominations to be making? What are the compelling theological images by which they carry out ministry and mission? Resources in UCGD: chapters 7-8 and 16.

### For Further Reading in This Area:

Wade Clark Roof, *Community and Commitment: Religious Plausibility in a Liberal Protestant Church.* New York: Elsevier North-Holland, Inc., 1978.

John S. Savage, *The Apathetic and Bored Church Member.* Pittsford, NY: Lead Consultants, 1976.

## *Chapter 6   Something That Works*

### For Bible Study:

The importance of applying the gospel to specific human conditions is seen in the seven brief letters to churches in Revelation 2–3. The group can prayerfully consider the probable conditions that precipitated each letter. How would these letters read to churches in our times? to your church?

### For Group Discussion:

For some people, the identification of church and community types is most revealing. For others, the uniqueness of each situation seems more compelling than the common characteristics of a church type. This chapter was intended for those who find help in thinking about types of churches, without feeling that any given congregation or community will ever fit the model or the profile. Since this chapter has more usefulness in what it suggests for further study, additional readings are listed for groups who may wish to pursue the contextual types or congregation profiles.

**For Further Reading in This Area:**

Dan Baumann, *All Originality Makes a Dull Church.* Santa Ana, CA: Vision House, 1976.

Avery Dulles, *Models of the Church.* Garden City, NY: Doubleday, 1974.

Ezra Earl Jones, *Strategies for New Churches.* New York: Harper & Row, 1976.

Paul Minear, *Images of the Church in the New Testament.* Philadelphia: Westminster Press, 1960.

H. Richard Niebuhr, *Christ and Culture.* New York: Harper & Row, 1951.

Lyle E. Schaller, *Hey, That's Our Church!* Nashville: Abingdon Press, 1975.

## *Chapter 7    Leadership: A Good Word for Pastors*

**For Bible Study:**

In a negative contrast, the positive values of Christian leadership are affirmed in Matthew 23:1-12. Who creates the unreal expectations and fantasies for the religious leader? How can the pastor develop authenticity?

**For Group Discussion:**

*Believing in the church.*    What is the vision of the future for this congregation? Is that vision positive? Is it shared by pastor and people? Is that vision clearly articulated and raised up for all the people from time to time? Resources in UCGD: chapters 3, 9-13, and 16.

*Pastoral care.*    How sensitive is the congregation to needs for personal care? Do some members share with the pastor in the care of others? Is the same care extended to nonmembers? Will they be expected to join? Should they? Resources in UCGD: chapters 9-10 and 13.

*Faith in the middle.* Is it really possible to believe something completely for oneself, but not hope that others will believe it also? Does pluralism weaken faith? Should the pastor carry the burden of raising up "a compelling image"? Resources in UCGD: chapters 3, 13, and 15.

*Good management.* What kinds of battles happen in your congregation? On what basis are decisions reached? Are the final decisions related to the larger vision of the congregation? Resources in UCGD: chapters 8-10.

*Personal faith.* In what ways is the pastor seen as authentic? How can the members share in the pastor's strengths and compensate for the pastor's weaknesses? Must the pastor be a person in touch with the divine? Resources in UCGD: chapters 3, 8-9, and 13.

**For Further Reading in This Area:**

James D. Anderson and Ezra Earl Jones, *The Management of Ministry.* San Francisco: Harper & Row, 1978.

John C. Fletcher, *Religious Authenticity in the Clergy.* Washington: Alban Institute, 1975. See also other publications by Alban Institute.

## *Chapter 8    Facts, Faith, and Strategy*

**For Bible Study:**

Read together the call of the church to the ministry of reconciliation, 2 Corinthians 5:16-21. How does God show love? Who are included in "the world"? Mainline churches have not seen the great commandment as reason to withdraw from the world, but rather the church is in the world in the form of the servant, God's agent of reconciliation.

**For Group Discussion:**

This final chapter reflects the emotions and the decisions that must be faced in the light of declining membership in mainline churches. The group might consider the available information, the apparent choices for denominations and congregations, and their individual feelings in facing these decisions.

Where the book ends, the church begins. As strategies develop and plans take shape, denominational committees and congregational groups are invited to share these with the author through Editorial Department, The Pilgrim Press, 287 Park Avenue South, New York, NY 10010. In this way your applications of concepts become continuing research to inform the whole church. As you tell the ways in which this material has or has not been helpful to you, the information will be relayed to those most concerned with continuing research in the church. Together we may better deal with an unfolding future.